ME AND MY
BIG MOVE

Hi there!

Welcome to "the club of Big Movers"! This book will take you through all the stages of your adventure: A Big Move. And the fun part, this is a WORKBOOK! Grab your pencils and start drawing, writing, and scribbling to create your own Big Adventure!

How to use the book?

★ Each chapter has its own color; you can "work through the rainbow".

★ Collect photos, drawings, tickets, and glue them in the book or store them in the back pocket.

★ Use this book together with your parents/guardians and friends.

★ Keep track: when you are finished with a page, you can mark it on the last page of the book.

★ And don't forget to use the stickers and postcards!

We use these icons in the book to point out:

   ideas and tips

   mindfulness games or topics about emotions

   extra printables which you can find online @ www.meandmybigmove.com

IT'S TIME TO GIVE THE PENCIL TO YOU.

ENJOY CREATING YOUR BIG ADVENTURE!

THIS BOOK IS ABOUT

1. ME AND MY FAMILY
2. BEFORE I LEAVE
3. PREPARE AND MOVE
4. EXPLORE MY NEW PLACE
5. MY FEELINGS ARE MY GUIDE
6. MY FRIENDS FROM EVERYWHERE
7. MY ADVENTURES

1. ME AND MY FAMILY

NAME:

THIS IS ME AND MY BIG MOVE

THIS BOOK BELONGS TO

NAME:

I WAS BORN IN:

DATE OF BIRTH:

AGE:

E-MAIL ADDRESS:

MY NEW HOME IS IN

PLACE:

COUNTRY:

THE REASON WE ARE MOVING/HAVE MOVED:

WE ARE PLANNING TO STAY IN OUR NEW HOME FOR   (MONTHS/YEARS)

FAMILY TRAVEL JOURNAL

Where have you, your parents/guardians, and grandparents lived before? You can ask them and write it down on these pages. Which is their favorite place to visit? And which place would you love to visit as well? You can also point out these places on the **ME AND MY FAMILY** map.

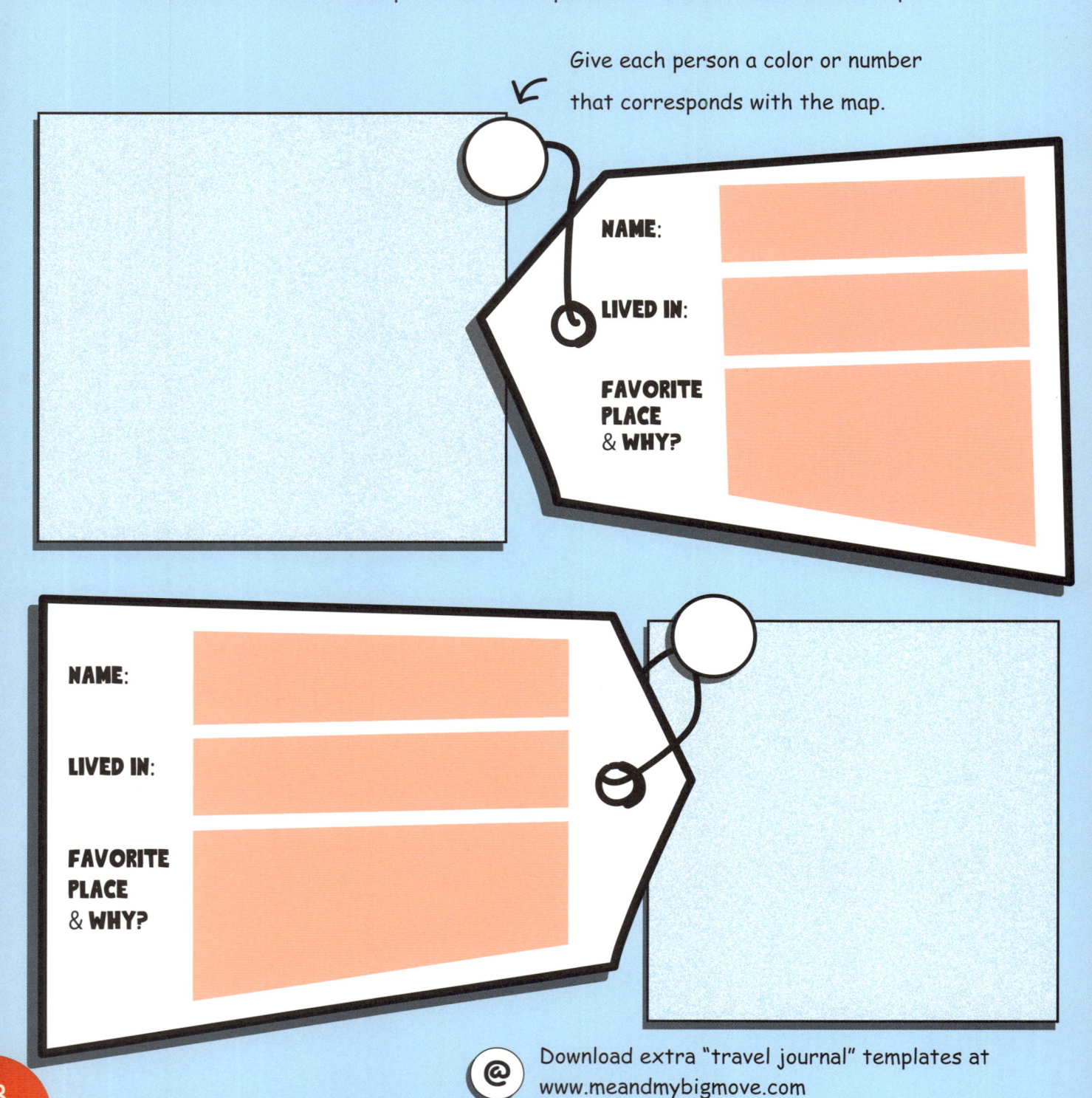

Give each person a color or number that corresponds with the map.

NAME:

LIVED IN:

FAVORITE PLACE & WHY?

NAME:

LIVED IN:

FAVORITE PLACE & WHY?

Download extra "travel journal" templates at www.meandmybigmove.com

ME AND MY FAMILY MAP

This is a world map of you and your family. How cool is that?! On this map you can label the places where you and your family members were born and the places they have all lived. Grab a sticker from the book or make simple signs like a dot or a star. Place these signs in the dotted circles. Use the same sign to mark the location on the map.

Here are some examples of how you can label them:

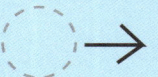

MAP KEY

- Here is where I was born
- Here is where I lived
- Here is where my mom was born
- Here is where my mom lived
- Here is where my dad was born
- Here is where my dad lived
- ....
- ....
- ....
- ....
- ....
- ....

I am moving with:

....

....

....

Who is moving with you?

Take a family picture, print it and place it here.

(You could also include your pets in the picture)

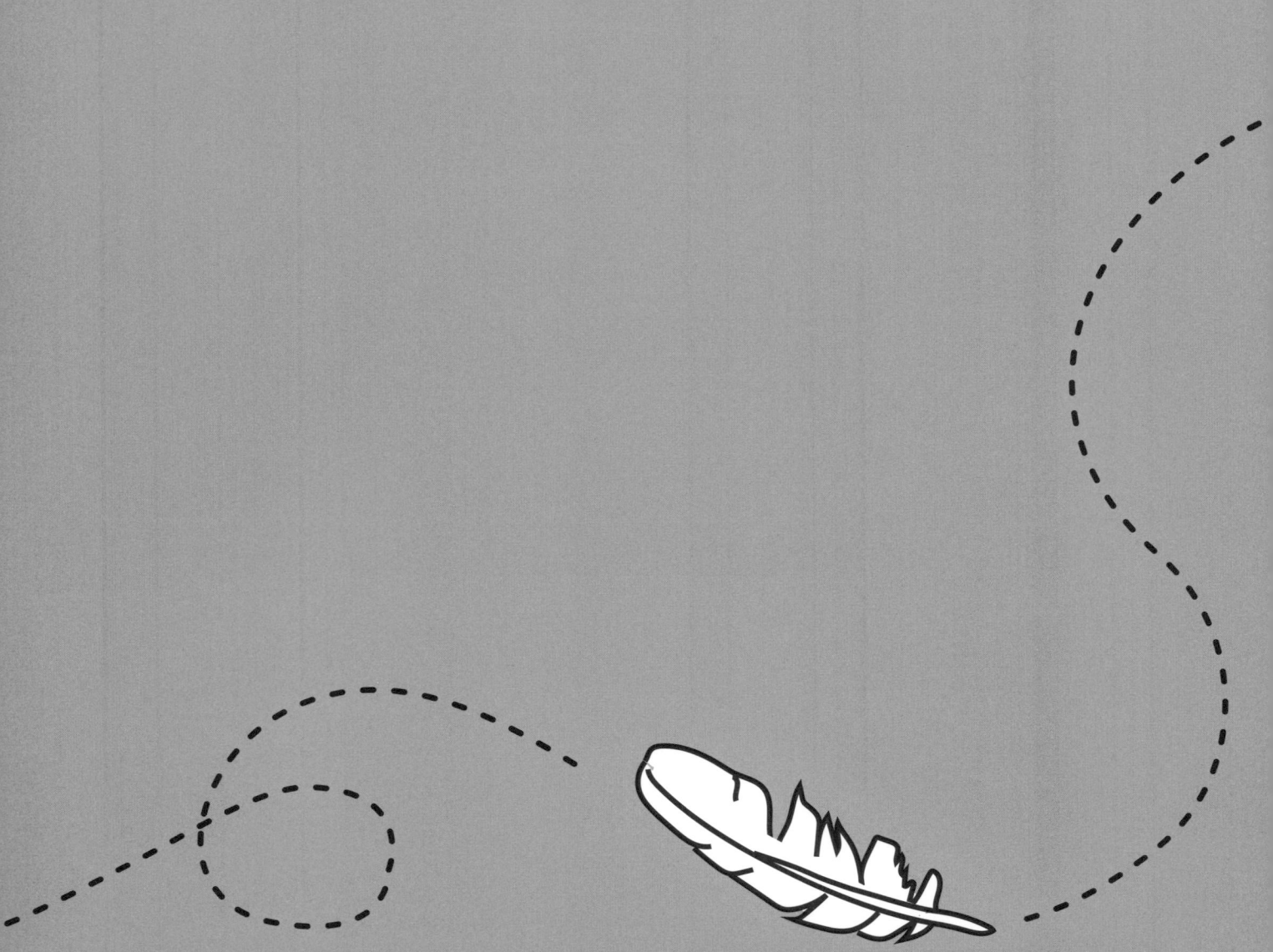

2. BEFORE I LEAVE

"I have twice as many friends now! Virtual and live friends. And with all of them I can play games on the computer."

Emma (11), Bristol to Rio de Janeiro

"I don't like to say goodbye to my friends. But I found out that it's not really a goodbye. With facetime it's so easy to call them."

Joshua (9), Prague to Oslo

"When my mom and dad told me we were moving from the UK to the Netherlands we got a camera to take all kinds of pictures of the places we loved here. We were moving back home and this way we could capture all of our favorite places. I still take a look in my photo album sometimes."

Jaap (8), Woking to The Hague

BEFORE I LEAVE

Do you know what it means to move from one place to another? Is this your first time relocating? Or have you lived in many other places before?

In this chapter you can list all the places you like to go and people you love to spend time with. The activities will help you say your "good goodbyes" to them and record it so you are always able to have a look at it later.

Saying goodbye can be tough. While working in this part of the book, you can experience a lot of different emotions. That is ALL OK! You can go to chapter five "My feelings are my guide" and complete an activity from that chapter. These activities can help you feel better!

MY FAVORITE PLACES

Where you live right now, has a lot of cool places to visit. A fun thing to do before you leave is to visit your favorite places one more time and record them in your book. First you need to decide which places you want to visit. A list can help you with that! Is it the nearest playground? The soccer field? A secret place of your own? Put it on the list here or create one yourself to hang in your room. Ask your parents/guardians or a friend to go there with you.

When you visit these places, you can take pictures and record them on pages 18 and 19. Write, draw, and glue pictures of your visit. And are there places you don't like to go? Write it all down. It will be fun to read this later!

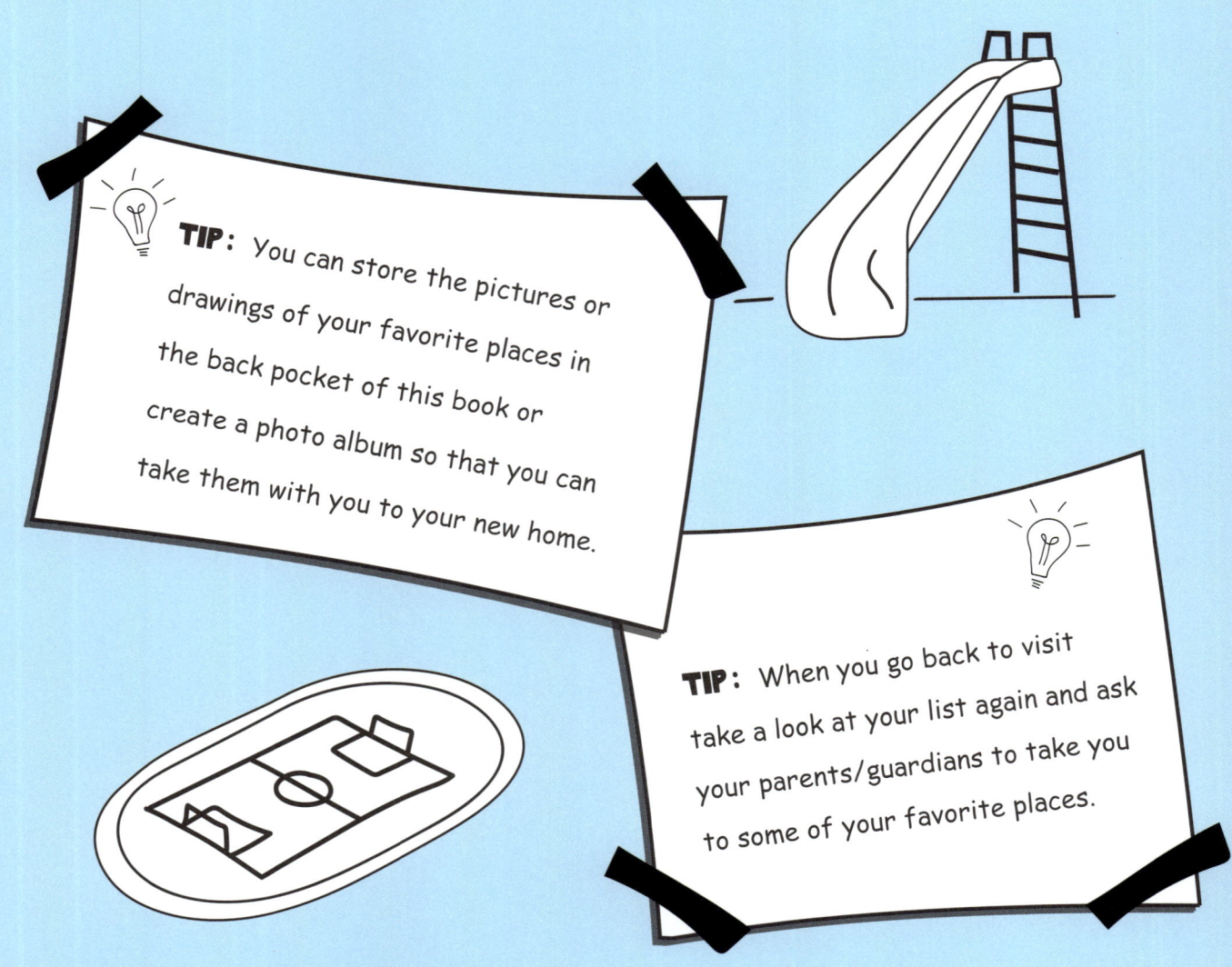

TIP: You can store the pictures or drawings of your favorite places in the back pocket of this book or create a photo album so that you can take them with you to your new home.

TIP: When you go back to visit take a look at your list again and ask your parents/guardians to take you to some of your favorite places.

My FAVORITE places list

1 ....

2 ....

3 ....

4 ....

5 ....

This is my list of places I would really like to visit before I leave.

 Want to hang a list in your room? Download "the favorite places list" at www.meandmybigmove.com

GALLERY OF MY FAVORITES

MY "GOOD GOODBYE"

Moving means saying goodbye to people. That is sometimes hard and it is ok to feel sad about it. Emily also felt that way when she moved from England to Brazil. Then she discovered a thing called "**GOOD GOODBYES**". She spent special time with the ones she loved, gave them an enormous hug and took pictures together with them which she hung in her new room. On page 22 you will find a list of ideas to create your own "good goodbyes". Have a look and write here how you prefer to say your "good goodbyes"!

My ideas for my "good goodbyes":

How do you feel today? Chapter 5 can help you guide your feelings. Take a look!

GOOD GOODBYES

Here is a list of ideas to create your "good goodbyes". You can mark or sticker the ones you have done in the checkboxes.

- [ ] Take pictures of the people you are leaving and put them in the back pocket of this book or give them a nice place in your new room.

- [ ] Choose a date to call them after you have arrived. Think about what time and day is best for both of you.

- [ ] Make a "goodbye bag" for friends and family. You can put pictures, drawings, a little gift, or a surprise in the bag.

- [ ] Make a necklace or bracelet together with a friend and swap them.

- [ ] Make a nice drawing for a friend or your grandparents.

- [ ] Choose a favorite spot and go there together and take "funny-face-selfies".

- [ ] Ask your friends to write on the "friend cards" in chapter 6 of this book.

- [ ] Leave a gift for a friend to open when you are away.

- [ ] Get special markers and paint a cushion, mug, or plate and give it to a friend.

- [ ] Create a treasure hunt! Hide a nice gift or letter in your surroundings and give the instructions to a friend just before you leave.

- [ ] _____

HOW DID YOU SAY YOUR "GOOD GOODBYE"?
Share it with us and we can share your great ideas with other little movers! Send a message to info@meandmybigmove.com

MY TREASURES

For a keepsake

Go and look for something small in or around your home that means a lot to you. It might be a rock, a feather, or a coin. Find a secret place around your home and tuck it in there as a way of leaving a part of yourself behind. And then walk around to find something small and special to you which you can take to your new home.

Make a treasure box

A treasure box can be made out of anything. It could literally be a box, but also a bag. You can decorate the box to make it extra special. Collect treasures you want to save as a memory from your current home. It can be photos of your home, your room, favorite teacher, or friends. A rock, a leaf, or a flower from a park. A bracelet, postcard, letter, or a coin. A part of something bigger that you can't bring along. A little bottle with sand from the beach or sandbox. Perhaps you receive some goodbye presents from your friends and family. You can also put them in your TREASURE box.

TIP Create a countdown calendar 3 weeks before the Big Move. Then you know when your box needs to be ready.

3. PREPARE AND MOVE

"When my mom and dad told me we were moving to Vancouver they read us a book about the country and the animals there. Did you know they have racoons, coyotes, and squirrels walking through the city? And even cougars and brown bears close to the city?! I was so excited when I found out about that!"

Jasmine (9), Paris to Vancouver

"The last weeks before the move we hung a big map of Dubai in the kitchen where the kids could look at and we could talk about the place we would be living soon."

Li Yong (38), Dad of 2, Hong Kong to Dubai

"Before we moved to Perth I had a zoom call with Maud, a German girl, who lives in Perth and I didn't know. It was a little bit scary to talk to her. But she told me how much she liked it in Perth and she said English is very easy to learn. When we arrived I met Maud and it was so much fun and great to have a friend at arrival."

Otto (6), Berlin to Perth

PREPARE AND MOVE

Your Big Move is right around the corner! It is almost time to start packing your things. In this chapter you will think about the things you would like to take with you to your new place. You will also learn more about the place you are going to be living soon. A good way to get a better image of your new place is to explore it before your arrival. How? You will discover it in this chapter. Have fun preparing and don't forget to take a picture on your moving day!

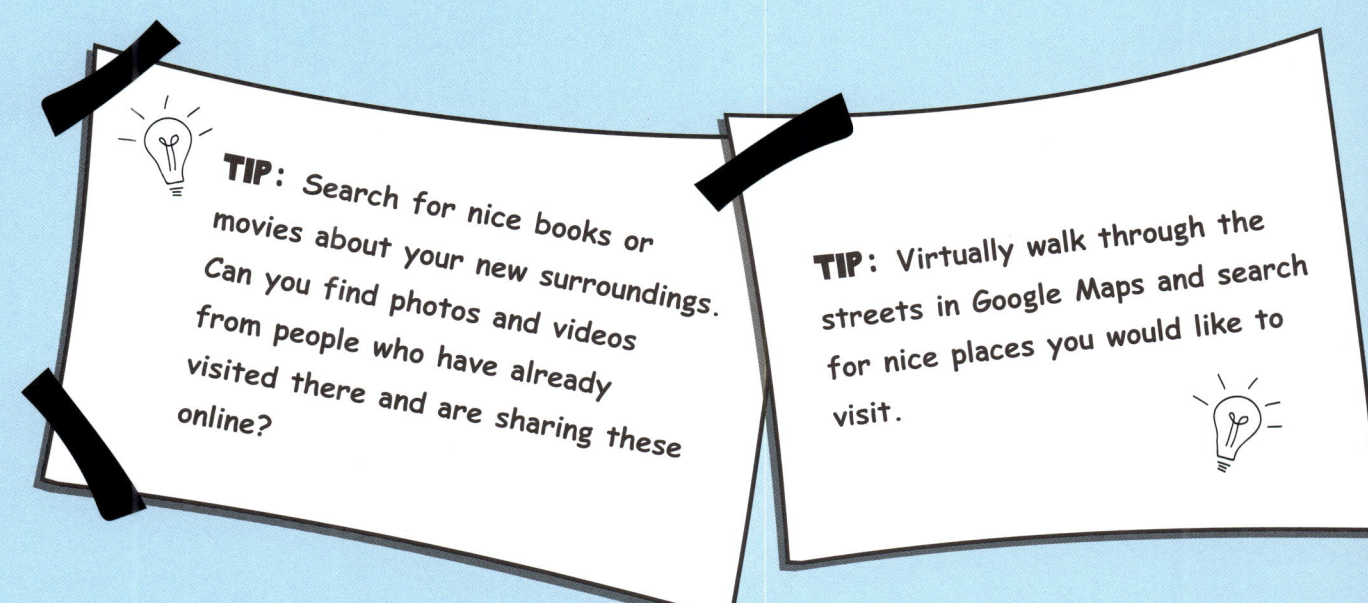

TIP: Search for nice books or movies about your new surroundings. Can you find photos and videos from people who have already visited there and are sharing these online?

TIP: Virtually walk through the streets in Google Maps and search for nice places you would like to visit.

PACK YOUR THINGS

Soon your things will be packed. Do you know what you can bring with you? If you only had one small suitcase to fill, what would you definitely like to bring? Tell your parents/guardians and ask if it is ok to bring these items. And if not, make pictures of them and place them here or in the back pocket of the book!

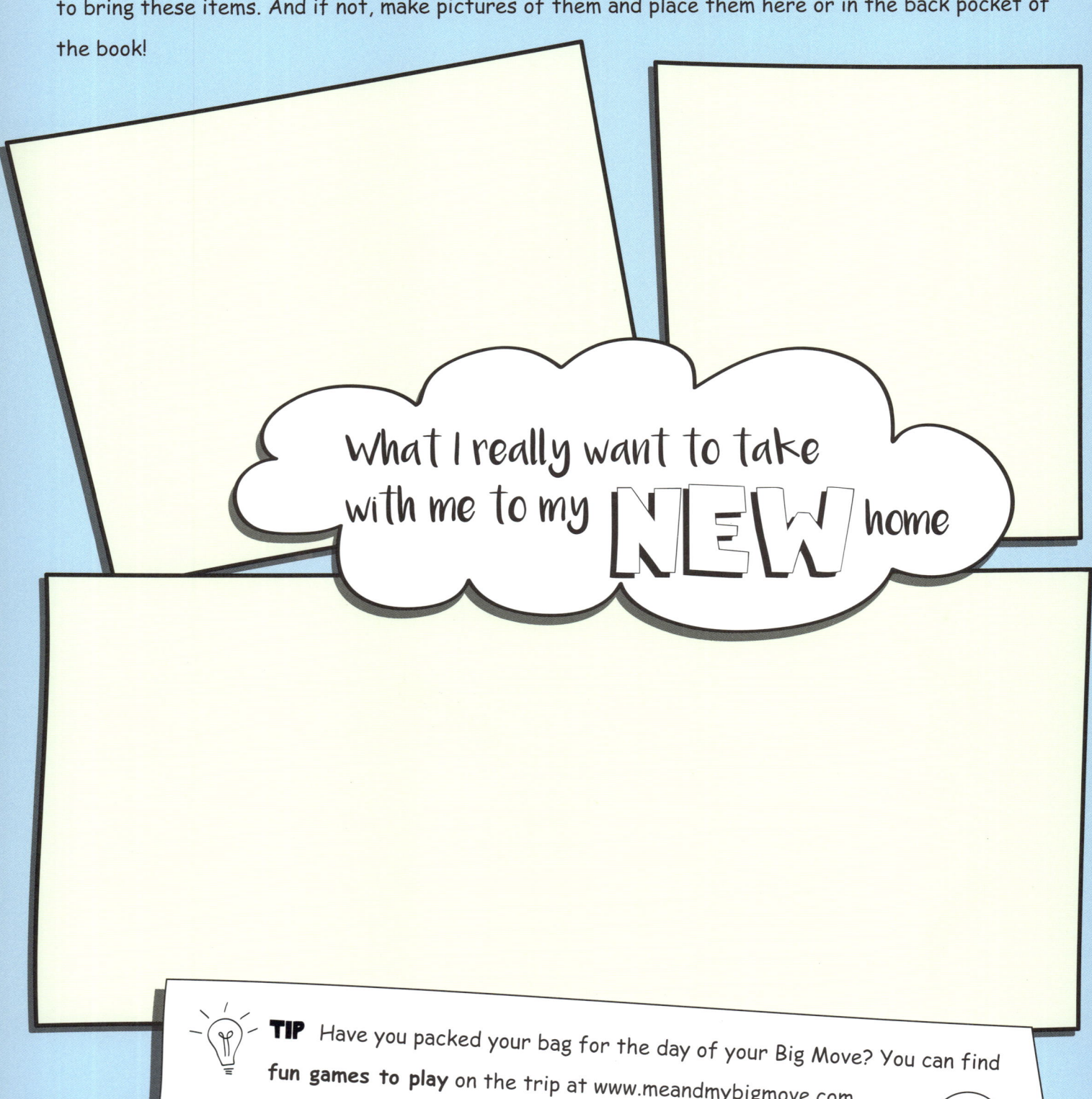

TIP Have you packed your bag for the day of your Big Move? You can find **fun games to play** on the trip at www.meandmybigmove.com

Investigate your new place

A good way to find out more about your new place is to ask someone who already lives there. You can ask an adult to help you arrange a virtual talk with a person who already lives where you will be living soon. When you talk with them you can ask questions about the topics you would like to know more about. For example: What is their favorite place to go to? What do they have for dinner? Or what is school like?

INTERVIEW with a local

Question: _____

Answer: _____

Question: _____

Answer: _____

Question: _____

Answer: _____

TIP: In your interview or at your new school ask what they do in the classroom and what songs they sing. You can listen and learn the song before your Big Move. This way you already know this before you arrive on your first day of school!

MY DISCOVERIES

This is what I discovered about my new living place!

I AM GOING TO:

THIS IS WHAT A COIN LOOKS LIKE:

THE FLAG OF MY NEW COUNTRY/STATE:

A FAMOUS BUILDING

I KNOW THESE WORDS IN MY NEW LANGUAGE:

Hello =

My name is =

Thank you =

Bye =

I am excited about

THE WEATHER:

Summer   Winter

sunny ☐   sunny ☐

cloudy ☐   cloudy ☐

rainy ☐   rainy ☐

windy ☐   windy ☐

MOST COMMON ANIMALS:

TIME ZONES

When you have a Big Move, it could be that you are going to live in a different time zone. A time zone is an area where everybody has the same time on their clock. The sun can't shine on all the places on Earth at the same time. So that means it is noon in one part of the world and at the same moment it is midnight in a different part of the world. That is why they came up with timezones. Some countries are so large that they have different time zones within their country!

You need:
* A clock with a white background
* Markers

CREATE YOUR OWN "TIME TO CALL CLOCK"!

Search for the timeframe which is best to call your friends and/or family members. Choose a color for this timeframe. Color in this timeframe at the background of the clock. When you are ready place the clock in your new home and you can easily see when you are able to chat with your friends.

Check www.meandmybigmove.com for a full tutorial of the "time to call clock".

1. WHAT TIME DO YOU WAKE UP IN YOUR NEW HOME?

TIME: ....

LOCATION: ....

2. WHAT WOULD THE TIME BE THEN IN YOUR PREVIOUS HOME?

TIME: ....

LOCATION: ....

1. WHAT TIME DO YOU GO TO BED IN YOUR NEW HOME?

TIME: ....

LOCATION: ....

2. WHAT WOULD THE TIME BE THEN IN YOUR PREVIOUS HOME?

TIME: ....

LOCATION: ....

Place a picture of your moving day.

MY BIG MOVING DAY

WE MOVED ON ............-............-................ (DATE)

THIS WAS A ....(DAY OF THE WEEK)

WE TRAVELED ....KILOMETERS/MILES TO GET TO OUR NEW HOME.

IT TOOK US ....HOURS TO GET HERE!

MY BIG MOVING DAY

Mark the place you left (with a sticker or your own symbol) and mark the place you are going to. Then create a dotted line between these places. This is the journey of your Big Move!

HOW DID YOU TRAVEL TO YOUR NEW PLACE?

What kinds of transport did you take to arrive at your new home?

How did your items travel?

4. EXPLORE MY NEW PLACE

"It is winter and Malika is chatting daily with her grandparents in the Netherlands. And every time during the call it is getting dark in the Netherlands and getting light in Seattle. Then one day Malika says: "Grandma, we are stealing your sun every day!" Since then they always make funny jokes of stealing each others sun."

Malika (5), Rotterdam to Seattle

"Each time we cycle along the river we see lots of turtles sitting on rocks. Yesterday I saw 15 turtles! I never saw turtles in the wild before!"

Katie (8), New York to Taipei

"I love it when we look out the window and play the game of "What do you see?" before bedtime."

Brandon (7), Manaus to Tokyo

EXPLORE MY NEW PLACE

Your new environment is probably different after your Big Move. Does it look different? Do people around you speak another language? Does it sound different when you walk outside? And what about the food? Is it tasty?

In this chapter we designed fun and mindful games you can play to explore your new environment by using your senses. We encourage you to go out with your family and enjoy new smells, discover new food, and take a look at your new school schedule. Take your time. There is a lot to discover. No need to do it all in one day :-).

The games in this chapter are located outside. Always ask your parents/guardians permission to go outside or ask them to come along. It is fun to do these activities together!

What is on your EXPLORING list?

A new place is very good for exploring. Do you already know where to go and what you would like to visit? For example a swimming pool or a playground? Write all these places on this list and try to find them in your neighborhood.

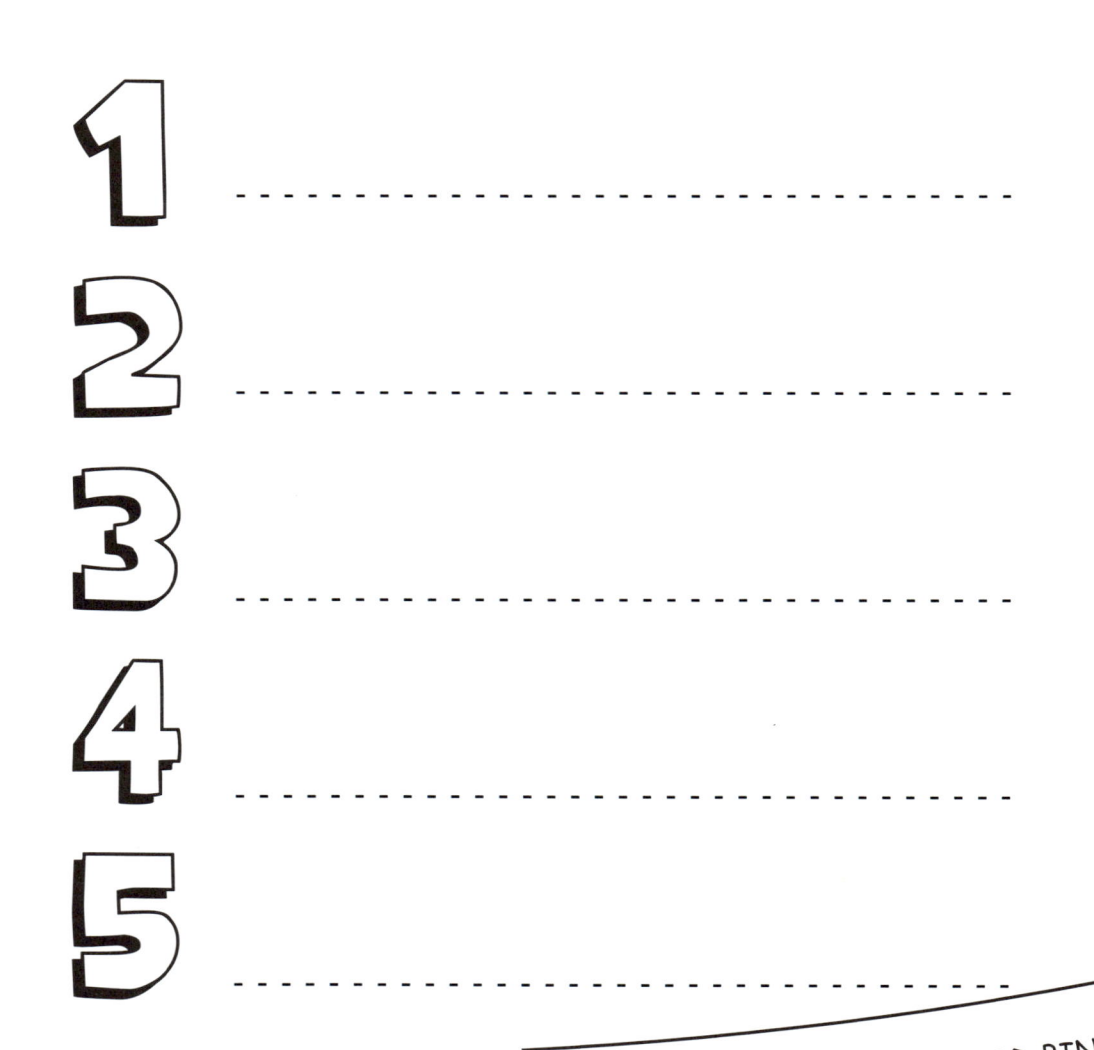

1 ....
2 ....
3 ....
4 ....
5 ....

@ Play the NEIGHBORHOOD BINGO to explore your neighborhood! Download this game at www.meandmybigmove.com

IN MY NEW HOME TOWN I DISCOVERED

Draw or write what you have discovered here. Think about places, people, food, games...!

My favorite place:

My WOW moment

USE YOUR SENSES
IN A MINDFUL WAY ♥

Sometimes when you are living in a new home, it can feel a bit strange. Does the sky look different to you? Or do you hear sounds you have never heard before? Do people speak with a different accent? Does the food smell funny? Does the wind feel chilly on your skin? You can feel a bit different in your new home not knowing why. That is all OK!

Do you know how this works? Every person has 5 senses that we use. We look at places with our eyes, we taste food with our mouth, we hear sounds with our ears, smell with our noses, and feel with our skin. Because we do that every day, we are so used to our surroundings that when we are in a new place, all of our senses will notice that!

We designed lots of games to discover your new surroundings by using your senses. Have fun!

GAME CAN YOU CONNECT EACH PICTURE WITH THE CORRECT WORD?

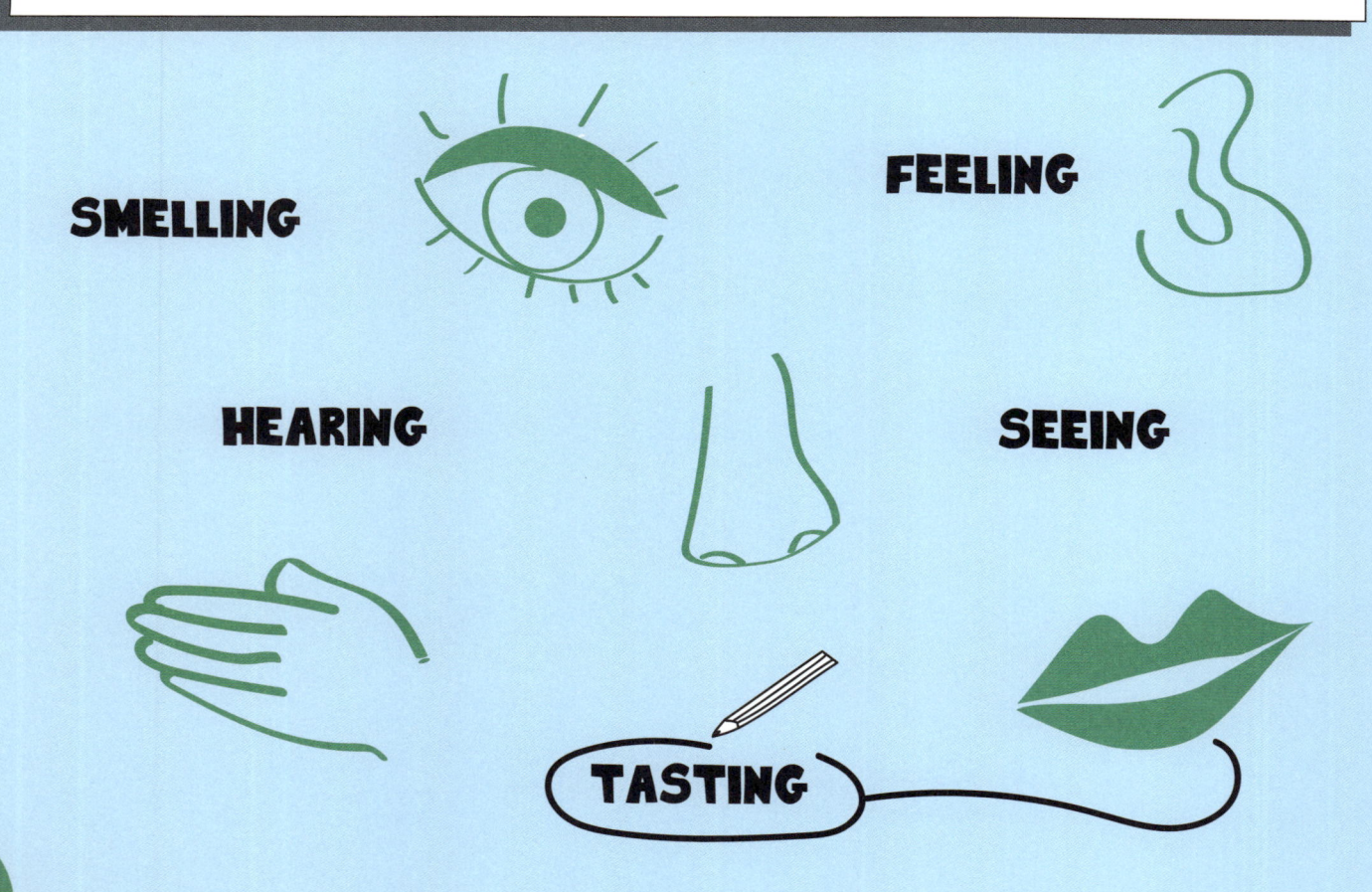

SMELLING   FEELING

HEARING   SEEING

TASTING

EXPLORING GAMES

WHAT DO I HEAR?

Take a recording device with you and go for a walk outside to explore the SOUNDS. Record five different sounds you hear along the way, and listen to them when you are back home. (No device? Take a notebook with you.) **What did you hear?**

What is different from your former place? What do you like or dislike?

WHAT DO I SMELL?

Go for a walk outside to explore the SMELLS. For example you can go to a local market, a bakery, or a shop. Try to define the things you smell. Describe two different kinds of smells here:

1 _____

2 _____

Does it smell different and do you like it? Write the type of smell you like and dislike here.

I LIKE: **I DON'T LIKE:**

NEED A BREAK DURING EXPLORING?

FIND A BENCH AND DO THIS EXERCISE!

Set a timer for 1 minute and sit in a calm body. Put your hands on your lap and close your eyes. Now listen to all the sounds around you. **What do you hear nearby? What do you hear further away? Can you hear sounds in your own body?**

BE THE GUIDE FOR ONE DAY

Ask your parents/guardians to go for a walk or bike ride to explore your new place. **You will be the guide for today!** When you want to go left, you all go left. When you want to go right, everybody goes right. You decide today!

this way!

THE COLOR WALK

Go for a walk to explore the COLORS outside. List the different colors you find during the walk, or take a camera and make pictures. On page 45 you can color the colorbox with the color you found. Write down, draw, or glue a picture of what you discovered in that color.

@ You can download extra "color walk" templates at www.meandmybigmove.com

USE AN EGG CARTON

Another way to explore your colorful place is to take an egg carton and paint each cup in a different color. Each little spot now has one color. When you go outside you collect colorful items like leaves, stones, or flowers. Put them in the right box. **Which box is full? Which one is not?**

MY COLOR WALK

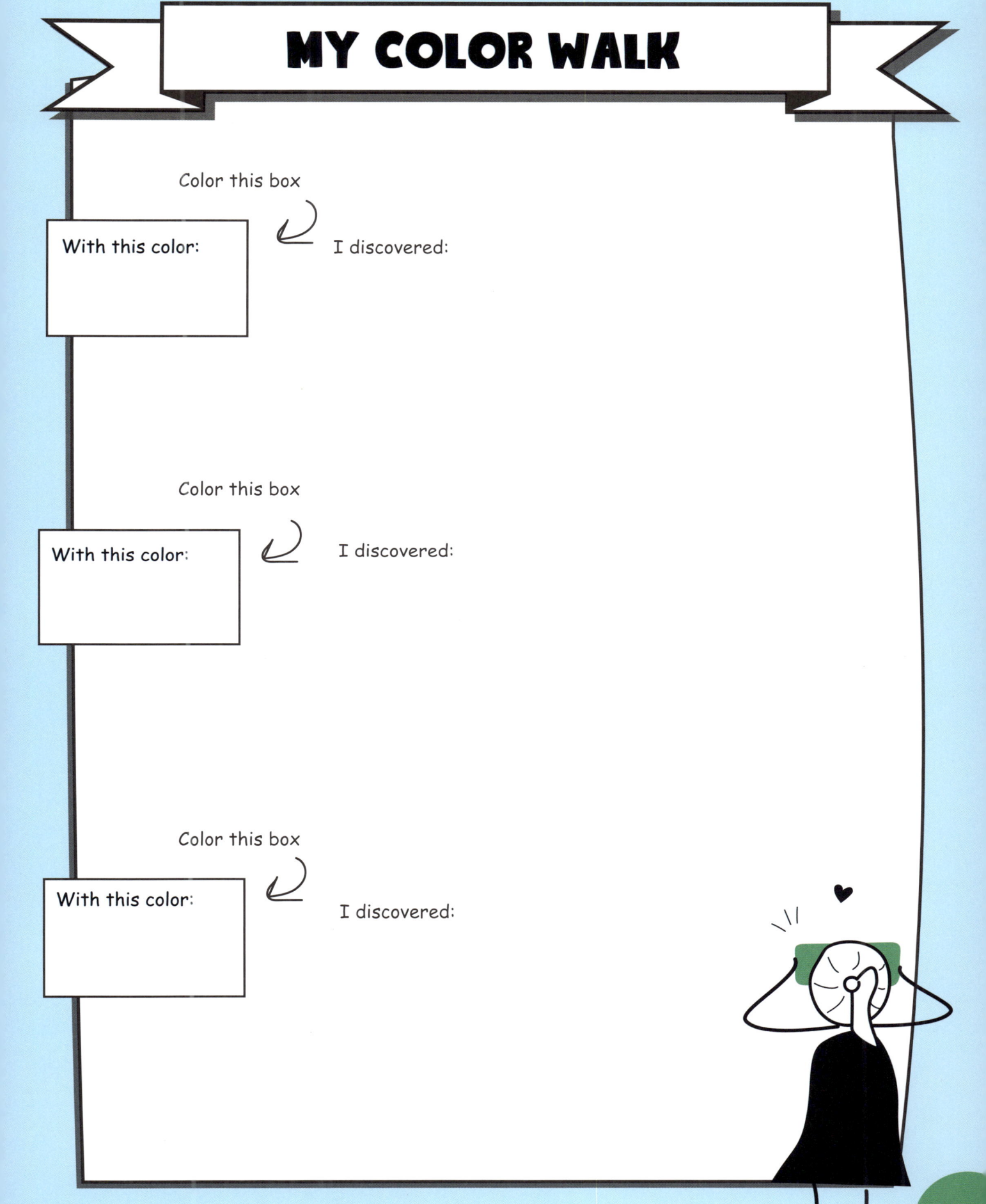

Color this box

With this color:

I discovered:

Color this box

With this color:

I discovered:

Color this box

With this color:

I discovered:

How does it LOOK?

When you walk through your new neighborhood, how does it look?

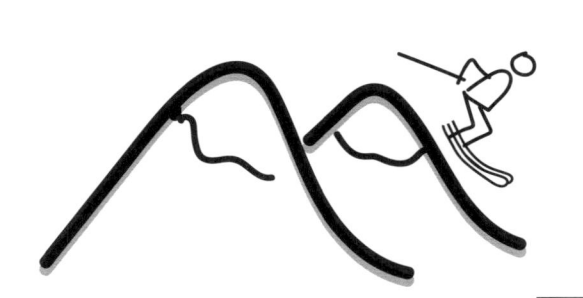

There are mountains  ☐   There is a forest ☐

There is a beach 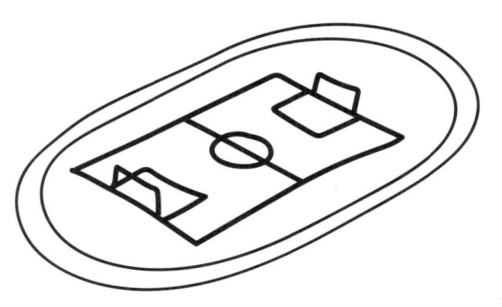 ☐   There is a sports field ☐

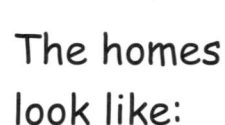

There is a playground ☐

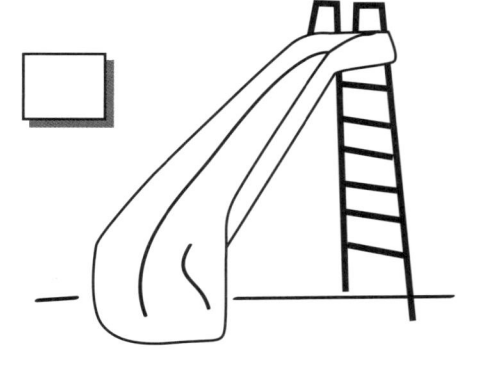

The homes look like:

☐ ... or  ... ☐ ... or ... _____

THIS IS MY NEW HOME

Draw your home here:

GUESS IT!
I THINK MY HOME IS:

AGE:

....................years old

SIZE:

..................meters/feet high

..................meters/feet long

..................meters/feet wide

CAN YOU GUESS THE SIZE OF YOUR NEW HOME?

Stand up and take one big step. Measure your step with a ruler. How big is 1 step?

If you take steps from one side of your home towards the other side. How many steps did you take? Write it down and fill in the sizes.

@ Did you already download the NEIGBORHOOD BINGO to play? Check www.meandmybigmove.com

MY DAILY ROUTINES

When you are settling in in a new place it is good to create new daily routines and keep up with your old ones. Routines can help give you structure and feel OK in your new home. We have created some daily routines especially for you to try. These mindful games can help you calm your mind and body. Keep it simple and start small. You can start right away!

MY GRATITUDE THOUGHTS

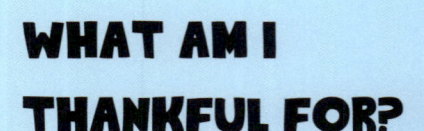

WHAT AM I THANKFUL FOR? ♥

Name 1-3 things you are thankful for.
Draw a picture or write them down on a small piece of paper or a sticky note.
Place them in a box or in your room.
Hard to draw? Say them out loud or whisper them. It is up to you what feels best!

THE TOP AND FLOP ♥ of the day

At dinner, ask everyone at the table to share their "TOP" (highlight) and their "FLOP" (a struggle) of that day. You will be surprised about the funny stories you might hear. Try it! It gets easier everyday.

💡 To create a ROUTINE try doing these activities on a specific moment every day. For example in the morning right after waking up, before dinner, or before bedtime. Keep it up for a longer period and it will become your new routine! You can do it! It is FUN.

EXPLORE YOUR PLACE BY NIGHT
What do you see or hear?

1 Put on your pajamas and make sure you do all your normal rituals.

2 Make it dark in your bedroom and look out the window.

3 What do you see? What can you hear?

Draw the view here. If you don't have a view from your bedroom window, choose a different room with a view.

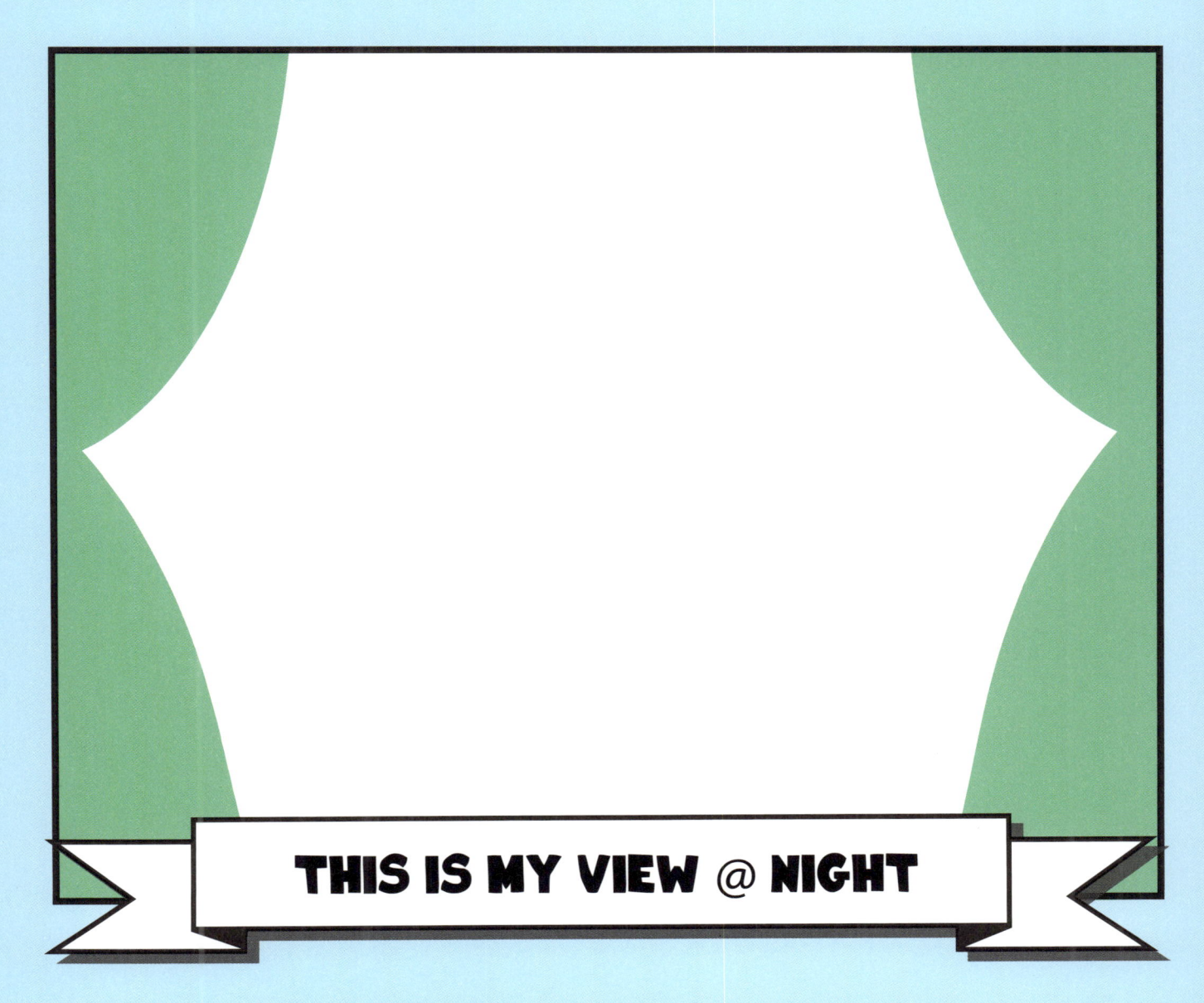

THIS IS MY VIEW @ NIGHT

If you like to draw more views you can download extra templates at www.meandmybigmove.com

MY FIRST WEEK AT SCHOOL

A Big Move means you are going to a new school! Are you excited about it? It is good to prepare yourself for your first week of school! Do you already know what your week will look like? On these pages you can fill in the activities in your new schedule. Think about: What time do you need to get up? What time do you leave the house? What time does school start? Do you have lunch there? Try to find the answers and write it in your new scedule here.

Wake up!

Lunchtime

School is out!

MONDAY

MORNING ACTIVITIES:

AFTERNOON ACTIVITIES:

AFTER SCHOOL:

TUESDAY

MORNING ACTIVITIES:

AFTERNOON ACTIVITIES:

AFTER SCHOOL:

I am excited about:

WEDNESDAY

_____

MORNING ACTIVITIES:

AFTERNOON ACTIVITIES:

AFTER SCHOOL:

THURSDAY

_____

MORNING ACTIVITIES:

AFTERNOON ACTIVITIES:

AFTER SCHOOL:

FRIDAY

_____

MORNING ACTIVITIES:

AFTERNOON ACTIVITIES:

AFTER SCHOOL:

I will go to my new SCHOOL by

Car ☐

Bike ☐

Bus/ school bus ☐

Foot ☐

Other:

TIP: Visit your new school before the first day. Can you find pictures online? Map out the best route to school and take this route together with your parents/guardians.

MY FIRST DAY @ SCHOOL

How was your first day at your new school?

NAME OF MY SCHOOL: ....

NAME OF MY TEACHER: ....

CLASS / CLASSNAME: ....

I AM SITTING NEXT TO: ....

MY FAVORITE PART OF THE DAY WAS: ....

MY FAVORITE PART OF THE LUNCHBREAK WAS: ....

....

....

THE GAMES I PLAYED: ....

....

WHAT MADE ME LAUGH ON THE FIRST DAY: ....

....

....

WHAT IS DIFFERENT AT MY SCHOOL: ....

....

....

IF I COULD BE THE TEACHER TOMORROW, I WOULD: ....

....

....

TRY NEW FOOD

1 Visit a grocery store, market, or look in the fridge. Choose 3 food items you know and 3 food items you don't know (yet).

2 Make a "try out" plate with these 6 items. Put very small pieces of each item on the plate. Write them on the review chart on page 55.

3 Take a bite and rate the food on a scale from 1 to 5. Five being very yummy and one being yucky. After finishing the plate, fill in your food scores.

LIKE A CHALLENGE? Put a napkin over the food and try it without seeing it. Do you dare?

TRY MINDFUL EATING ! Wait to take the first bite. Look at it. What is the color and structure? Now smell it. Now only touch it with your tongue. What do you feel, do you already taste something? Finally have a slow-motion bite and now again describe the texture and taste. How does it feel in your mouth? Is it tasty? Share what you all discovered. High five! You did it!

Draw your favorite food on the plate.

my favorite meal

MY FOOD REVIEW

Food:

My score:

☆☆☆☆☆
☆☆☆☆☆
☆☆☆☆☆
☆☆☆☆☆
☆☆☆☆☆
☆☆☆☆☆

WHAT I REALLY LIKE:

WHAT I DIDN'T LIKE THE FIRST TRY:

WHAT I WANT TO TRY AGAIN:

Want to do a "food review" together?
Download extra templates at www.meandmybigmove.com

EXPRESS YOURSELF

Sign language can help you communicate with other people. It is a fun hands-on language. When you are in a new place you may not have the words to make yourself clear. Having signs to rely on gives you another option to communicate with your new friends. Once you (and maybe your friends) have mastered a few signs, you will be able to express yourself. Give it a try!

FUN GAME: Try out some of these signs together with your friends. Maybe you need some help from an adult to translate. **Try to create some signs together and they can become your secret signs!**

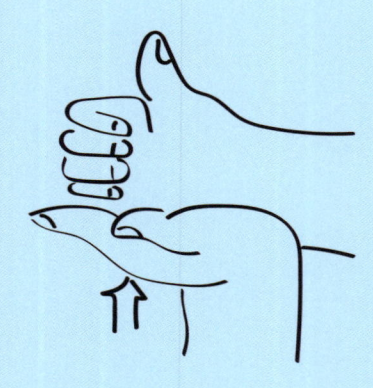

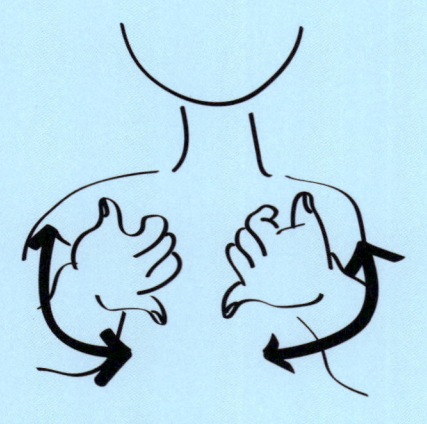

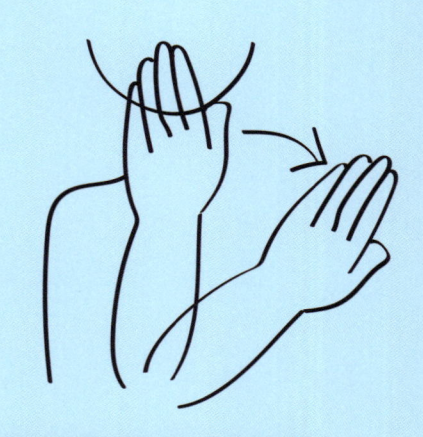

HELP   PLAY   THANKS

>> These signs are examples from American Sign Language.

> **TIP**
> If you are in a situation and you don't know the words to explain (yet).
> Try to show it by using your body language to explain what you mean.

NOTE FOR THE PARENTS/ GUARDIANS

Help your child learn a few words in sign language. Start with simple words like hello, bye-bye, my name is [NAME] and incorporate feelings into the mix like proud, mad, and happy. Always support sign language with the spoken language. It's likely that other children will not know sign language, and of course your child will eventually have to speak the words. But it is a good start to feel more comfortable in a new environment. Tell the teacher at school the signs you learned so they understand the meaning as well.

FIRST WORDS

My first words in my new language are:

DRAW IT!

If you don't know the words yet, you can try drawing it! What does: "I need to go to the toilet" look like? You can draw a toilet. Or you can draw a glass of water for..."I am thirsty?" Try some here.

58

5. MY FEELINGS ARE MY GUIDE

"Sometimes I cry when I hear a song about friends, because I miss them. Then my mom always gives me a very big hug and we sing the song together. I like that."

Sarah (7), Orlando to Portland

"One of the best things I learned from relocating to a totally different environment is that you can feel a lot of emotions you never felt before. Growing up I never really learned to talk about my feelings. I would like to tell every child and parent: IT IS ALL OK! Don't try to take it away. Let it be there and let it guide you."

Mariana (40), San Louis to Queenstown

"I don't like to be far away from my friends and I hate talking about how I feel about this. After my dad asked me to play a game about "faces and parts of your body" we laughed a lot. It made it easier for me to tell him how I felt."

Marco (11), Milan to Houston.

MY FEELINGS ARE MY GUIDE

Emotions are a part of you. We all have them. We cry when we feel sad, we smile when we are happy, and our stomach may feel upset when we are a bit anxious. By showing our emotions in expressions on our face, or in the way we behave, we let other people know how we feel. And that can be very helpful. So express them!

You can feel one emotion or you can feel several at the same time. Emotions are like waves at the sea. They come and go. They may surprise you sometimes. That is OK. By letting them be there they become part of you and they will guide you.

Sometimes it is good to pause and listen to what an emotion is telling you. In this chapter we designed activities for you to discover everything about your feelings. Don't forget to share all kinds of emotions with your loved ones. Enjoy the activities!

FEELINGS IN YOUR BODY

The child in the picture is feeling anxious and stressed. He knows this because he can feel this emotion in several parts of his body. Do you recognize this feeling? Can you recall a moment when you have experienced this?

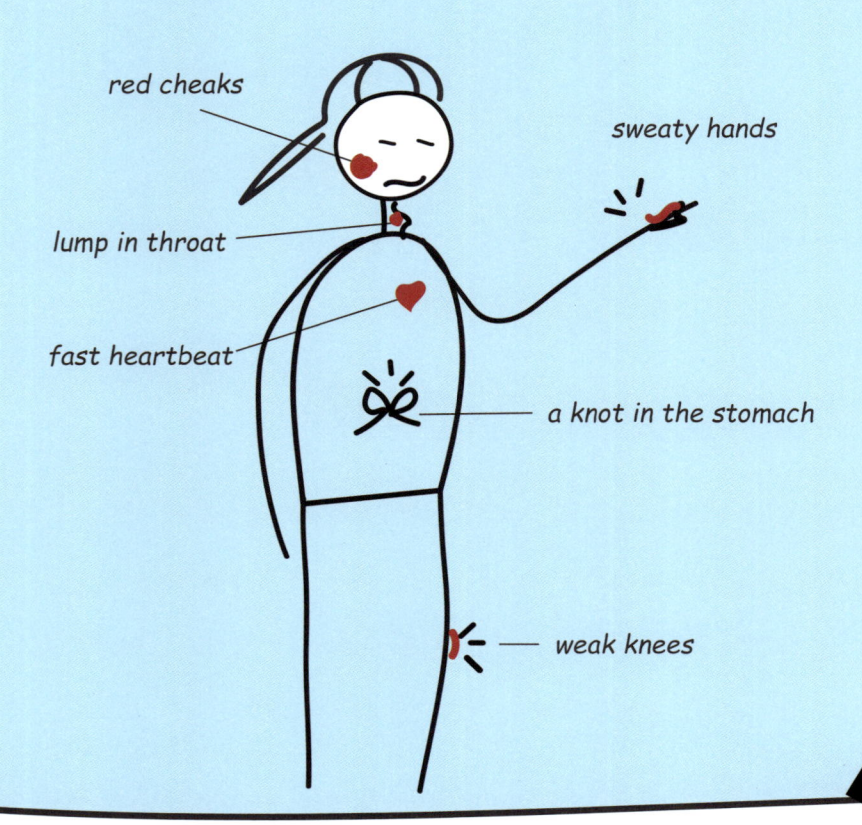

- red cheaks
- sweaty hands
- lump in throat
- fast heartbeat
- a knot in the stomach
- weak knees

YOU ARE BRAVE! ♥

Most of us experience the feeling of being anxious about certain things. This can happen when we try out new things or speak in front of a big group. Our body gives signals to let us know that we feel anxious. It helps to say to yourself:

If I am feeling anxious, then I must be about to do something very brave!

WHAT DO I FEEL WHERE? ♥

We can recognize different kinds of emotions by feeling them throughout our body. On this page you can discover your emotions in your body. Give each box (eg happy, scared, etc.) a different color and color the part of the body where you feel these kinds of emotions.

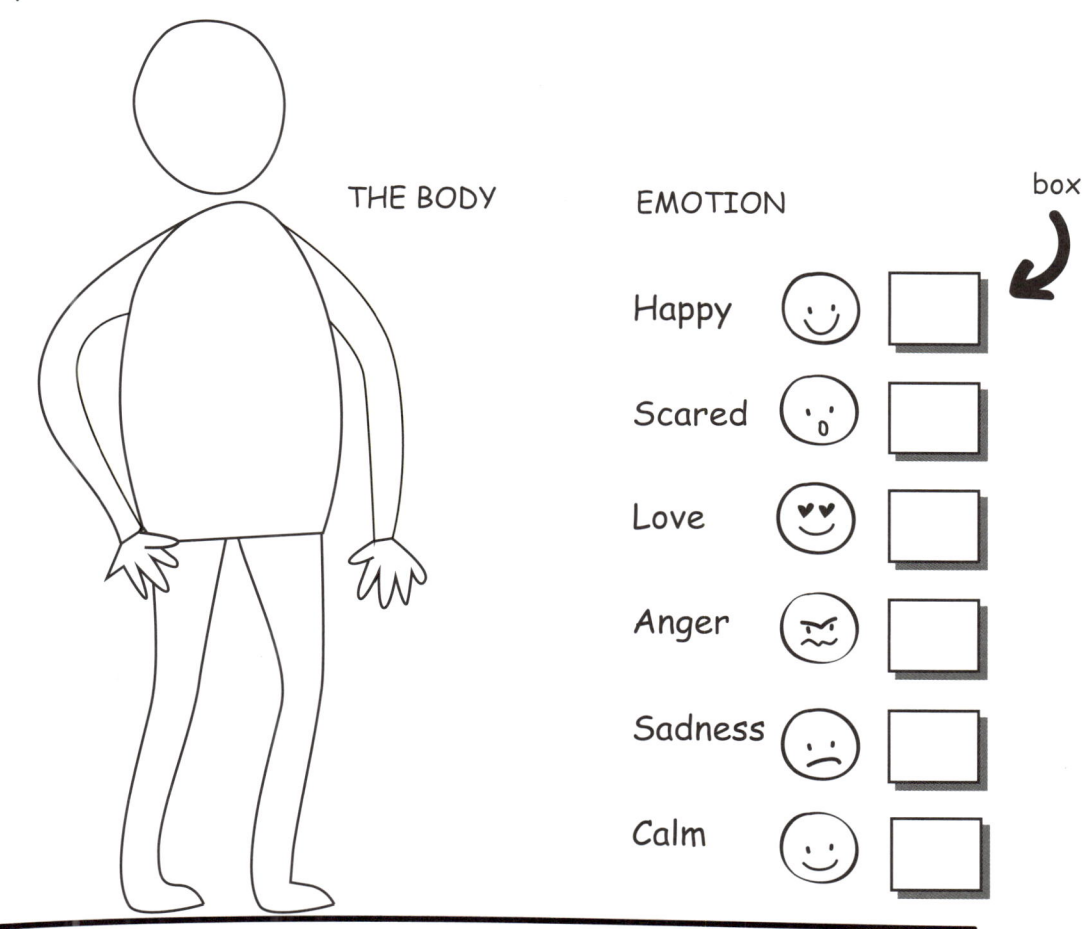

THE BODY

EMOTION — box

- Happy 🙂 ☐
- Scared 😮 ☐
- Love 😍 ☐
- Anger 😠 ☐
- Sadness 🙁 ☐
- Calm 🙂 ☐

BONUS QUESTION:

Where can you feel your breath?

Try it first and then turn this page upside down for the answer.

Answer: There are three places you can feel it: your belly, chest, and nose. Can you feel them all? Try it! Focusing on your breath can help you get calm. It is also a great tool to train your attention!

HOW DOES IT LOOK? ♥

Play this game with someone else. Make sure you can see and hear each other very well.

1 Close your eyes and point with one finger to one of the emotions on the page. Open your eyes to see which one you picked.

2 Stand up and EXPRESS this emotion. Try to use all parts of your body.
For example: you picked angry.
> What does angry look like?
> What do you do when you are angry?

3 The other person tries to guess which emotion you are expressing.

4 Were you able to guess them all correctly? Which was hardest to express? Which was easiest?

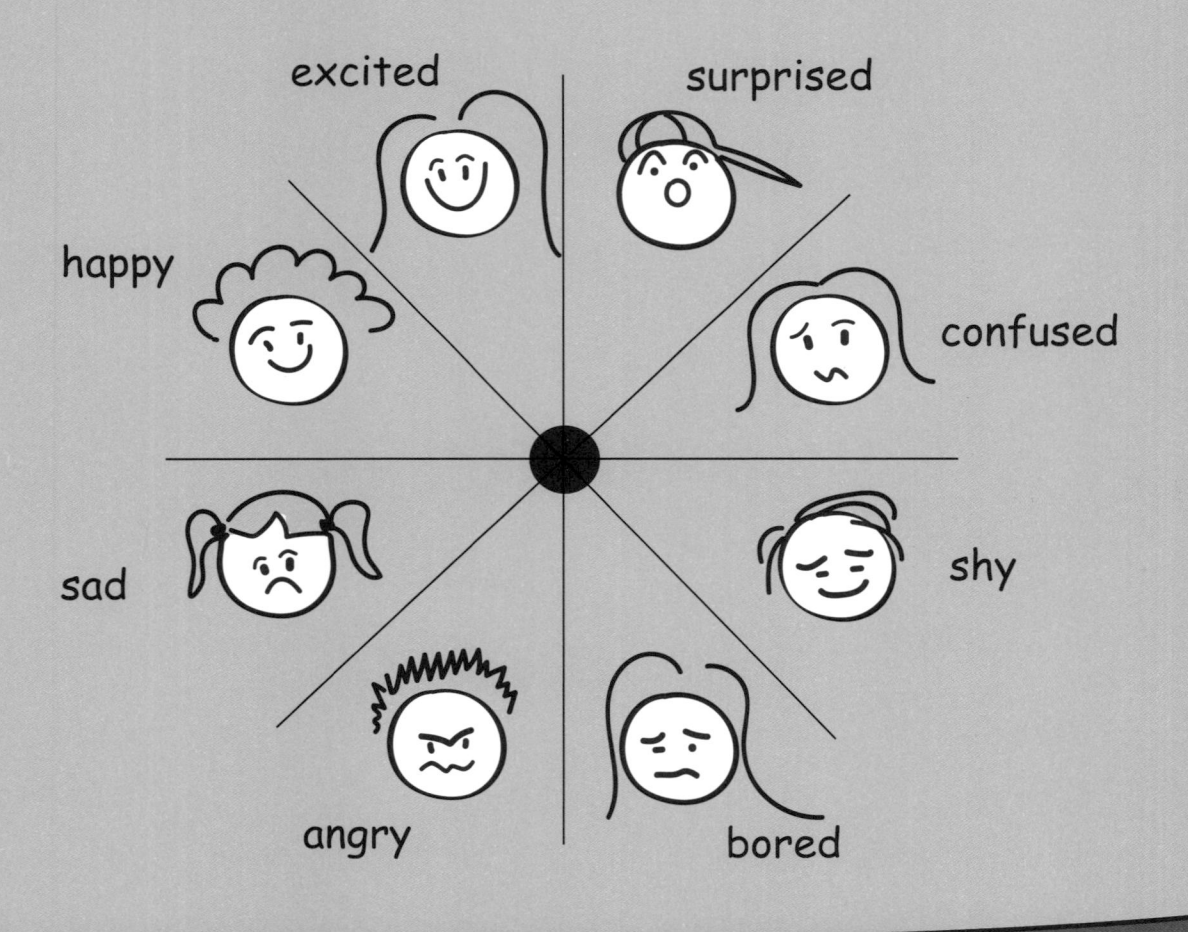

excited surprised
happy confused
sad shy
angry bored

MY GALLERY OF FACES ♥

In this gallery you can draw all your facial expressions! Think back to the kind of emotions you have experienced lately. Do you remember a specific moment and why you felt that way? You can draw your facial expression in one of the circles and write the moment down on the dotted line. No need to fill them all in at once. You can return to this page at any time.

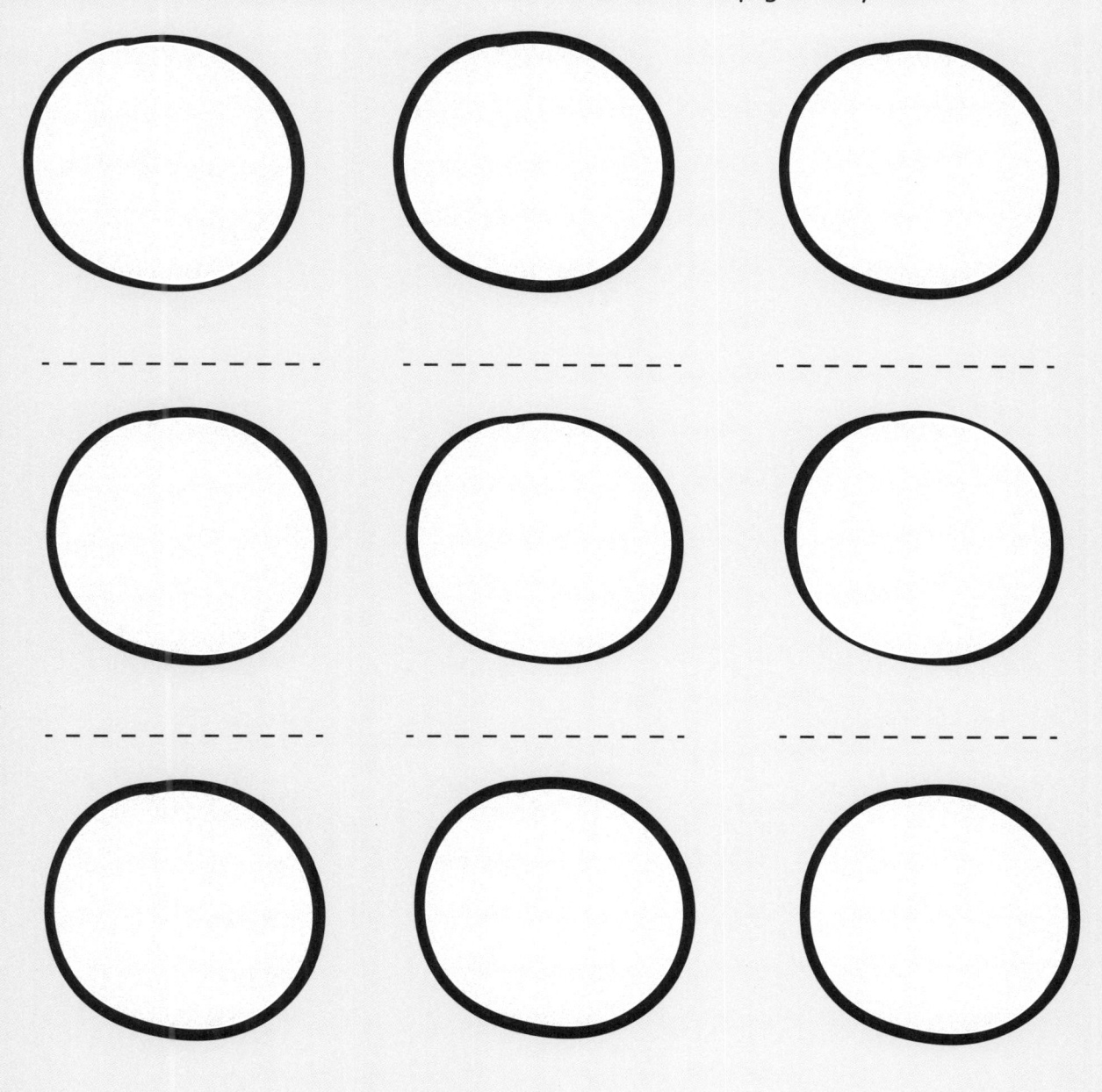

TIP: Together you can have fun drawing the facial expressions of the other. Ask them why they looked that way at that moment.

You can download extra "faces" at www.meandmybigmove.com.

MY HELPERS ♥

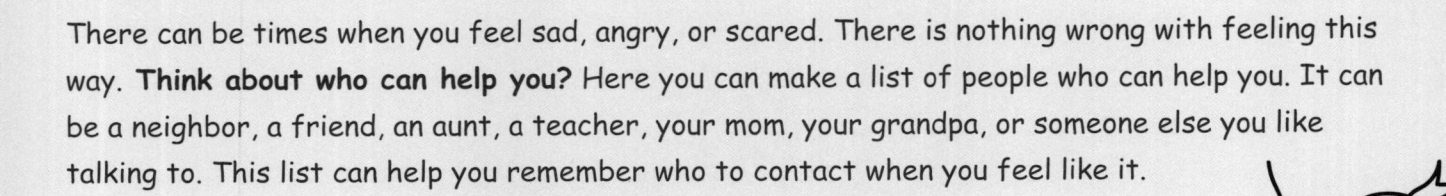

There can be times when you feel sad, angry, or scared. There is nothing wrong with feeling this way. **Think about who can help you?** Here you can make a list of people who can help you. It can be a neighbor, a friend, an aunt, a teacher, your mom, your grandpa, or someone else you like talking to. This list can help you remember who to contact when you feel like it.

My helpers are:

You can also help yourself! There are simple ways you can help yourself feel happier or calm again. Think of small activities that make you feel better, such as squeezing a stress ball, stamping your feet ten times, dancing to your favorite music, creating a drawing, or getting a big hug. You can make a list here and share it with your parents/guardians or with a helper from your list. They can remind you of these activities when you need it.

This activity makes me feel better:

I AM GOOD AT: ♥

Connect all the numbers and discover the shape. What is it? It is a: _ _ _ _ _ _

Now you can use the image by writing what you are good at on the dotted lines. It is not only about what you have achieved. It can also be about being kind, being a good friend, being helpful at home, or doing your best at school. **What are you good at?**

I AM A SUPER ADVENTURER!

One of the best things about living in a new place is that you get to try new activities. What are the new things that you have tried? Draw or write down the things you have tried and learned since your arrival. WOW that is amazing!

BEING SUPER KIND ♥

Being super kind means being willing to share and help others. Here are some examples of how you can be SUPER KIND: create a gift, make a drawing, send a postcard, or bake cookies and share them. You can say "thank you" when someone helps you or say "please" when you ask for help. **Think about: How were you kind today? What can you do for someone else tomorrow?**

Sometimes during a Big Move, you can have lots of thoughts in your head. If you can't sleep, it could be that you are feeling a bit scared about something or feeling worried. Mr. Wind is here to help you! Give your thoughts and worries to him. Draw or write them in these clouds and blow them away with Mr. Wind.

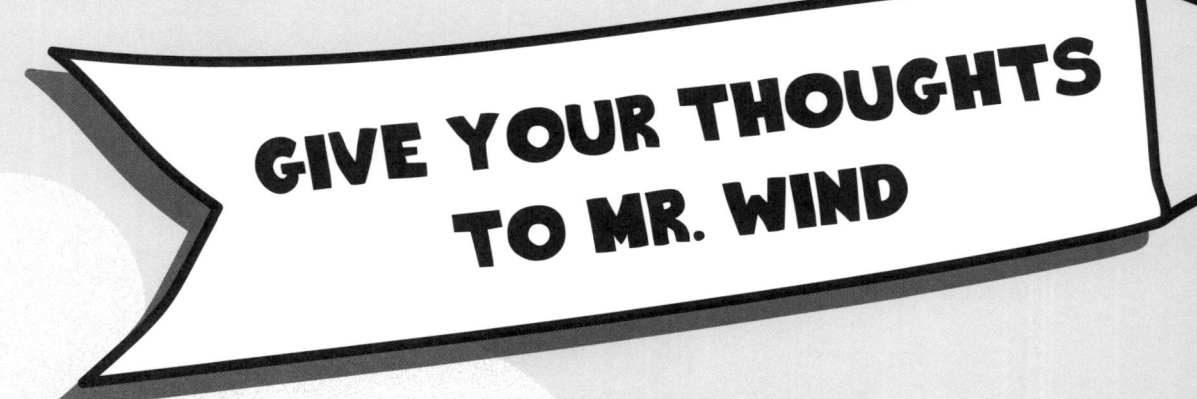

Take a deep breath and ......PPFFFFFFFFFFFFFFFFFFFF!!!

GIVE YOUR THOUGHTS TO MR. WIND

MR. WIND

BREATHING EXERCISES ♥

Feather breath
Hold a feather in front of your face. Then inhale and exhale through your nose. **Can you see the feather move?**

Shape Breath
Choose a shape like a square, triangle, circle or a star. Try to make the shape in the air by using one full breath. Start making a shape while inhaling and finish your shape as you exhale.
Which shapes were easy to make in one breath? Can you extend your breath to finish a difficult shape? WELL DONE!

6. MY FRIENDS FROM EVERYWHERE

"I love playing soccer. In my new town I could play soccer straight away. That was so cool! And my teammates are great. Every Saturday we play together after the game."

Oliver (11), Brisbane to Los Angeles

"Before my first day of school I had already met a girl from my new class. My mom arranged a play date for us. So when I had my first day of school, she came to greet me right away when I walked into the classroom. That was great!

Selma (10), Copenhagen to London

"I colored a postcard and sent it to my friend in Hong Kong. And he called immediately after receiving it! It was nice to talk again."

Roger (5), Hong Kong to Abu Dhabi

MY FRIENDS FROM EVERYWHERE

When you relocate you meet new people. Whether that is in your new neighborhood, at your new school, or while doing activities you enjoy. Making new friends might be a bit scary at first, but if you smile and say "Hi" to a new person, you will notice most of them will smile back at you :-).

Making new friends is a good way to have fun and feel at home in your new place. But it is also important to stay in touch with your old friends. In this chapter we share ideas on how to stay in touch with your friends and how to make new friends. You can log all your friends around the world on the world map and you can ask them to fill in a "friend card". Don't forget to ask them how to stay in touch! Is it a new play date next week or virtual bingo? Have a look at the tips on the next page. Have fun!

@ You can download extra "friend cards" at www.meandmybigmove.com.

IDEAS TO MAKE NEW FRIENDS

Are you excited to make new friends? Many other kids were happy to share their ideas with you! We listed the best ones for you here. You can take a look at this list with your parents/guardians and go for it. Remember, you are very brave!

- [ ] Visit a playground and introduce yourself to the other kids that are playing. Say: "Hi, I am (name) ....". If you find that a bit scary, you can practice a few times with a family member at home.

- [ ] Ask for a buddy at school. A few weeks before school starts, ask the school if they can help you meet a classmate before your first day of school.

- [ ] Join a group activity, for example a sports team, ballet class, art class, choir, or sign up for an activity at a local community center.

- [ ] Invite kids for play dates at your home. You can spend time with them in a safe environment. It will also help you to feel more comfortable at school.

- [ ] Bake some cookies or a cake and bring them to your new neighbors.

- [ ] Ask your parents/guardians to invite your neighbors (with kids) for a dinner or a housewarming.

- [ ] Try to learn a few words in your new language so you can greet people.

- [ ] Ask the people around you what the best places are to meet kids your age.

- [ ] Together with an adult, have a look on the Internet for community activities especially for kids.

My Friends Map

You can mark or write the homes of all of your friends on this world map. You can put a sticker, draw a circle with a number, or a name on the map where all of your friends live.

HOW TO STAY IN TOUCH

Enjoying making new friends doesn't mean forgetting your old friends. There are a lot of ways to stay in touch with your friends. Ask them for their contact information, like their address, phone number, or social media account. Write it here on the "friend cards". This way you are always able to contact them, to share a happy moment together or to talk when you are feeling sad. Because that's what friends are for! Here are some great ideas to stay in touch.

- ☐ Find out what time and day is the most convenient to call and put it on your calender. Ask an adult to help you make the call.

- ☐ Create a nice drawing or artwork, put it in an envelope and send it to your friend.

- ☐ Set a date to play an online game.

- ☐ Color in one of the postcards in this book and send it to your friend.

- ☐ Mark the birthdays of your friends on your calendar and send a message or video to congratulate them. Send it at the time they wake up.

BEING A TRUE FRIEND MEANS:

- ★ Being helpful
- ★ Sticking up for your friend
- ★ Supporting them
- ★ Listening well
- ★ Sharing with them
- ★ Being honest

@ You can download extra "friend cards" at www.meandmybigmove.com.

FRIEND CARD

NAME: _____

BORN IN: _____

LIVING IN: _____

HOW WE MET: _____
_____

HOW TO KEEP IN TOUCH?
_____
📞 _____

Age:
BIRTHDAY date
............../............../..............

FRIEND CARD

NAME: _____

BORN IN: _____

LIVING IN: _____

HOW WE MET: _____
_____

HOW TO KEEP IN TOUCH?
_____
📞 _____

Age:
BIRTHDAY date
............../............../..............

FRIEND CARD

NAME: _____

BORN IN: _____

LIVING IN: _____

HOW WE MET: _____

_____

HOW TO KEEP IN TOUCH?

_____

☎ _____

Age:

BIRTHDAY date
......../......../........

FRIEND CARD

NAME: _____

BORN IN: _____

LIVING IN: _____

HOW WE MET: _____

_____

HOW TO KEEP IN TOUCH?

_____

☎ _____

Age:

BIRTHDAY date
......../......../........

FRIEND CARD

NAME: _____

BORN IN: _____

LIVING IN: _____

HOW WE MET: _____

_____

HOW TO KEEP IN TOUCH?

_____

📞 _____

Age:

BIRTHDAY date
........../........../..........

FRIEND CARD

NAME: _____

BORN IN: _____

LIVING IN: _____

HOW WE MET: _____

_____

HOW TO KEEP IN TOUCH?

_____

📞 _____

Age:

BIRTHDAY date
........../........../..........

7. MY ADVENTURES

"It is so much fun when we have visitors because I get to be the guide for a day. I show them all my favorite spots and we eat out more often! I like that a lot."

Brian (6), San Fransisco to Boston

"When we moved to Curaçao I learned to snorkel. It is so beautiful to see all the fish swimming. And when my cousin came to visit I showed her all the fish. My favorite is a clownfish."

Stijn (8), Amsterdam to Willemstad

"I don't get to see my grandparents every week anymore, but now we make these amazing long trips together when they come to visit us."

Aakash (6), Dehli to Jakarta

MY ADVENTURES

Moving to another place can be a big adventure. Everything is new and it can be really exciting to go on day trips, weekend adventures, and/or holidays to different places than you are used to. This chapter is for you to treasure all of your lovely trips.

There may be friends and family members coming to visit you, your family, and your new home. Ask your visitors to write a small story on your guestbook pages. It will be fun to read later!

@ You can download extra "guestbook templates" at www.meandmybigmove.com

TRAVEL JOURNAL

Where did you go? On these signposts you can write the names of all the trips you made and on the next pages you can record your trips. **What did you like? Did something funny happen?**

MY TRIP TO:

FROM ................-................-................ (DATE)

TO ................-................-................ (DATE)

I WENT WITH ....(PERSONS)

THE WEATHER WAS:

- Sunny ☐
- Cloudy ☐
- Rainy ☐
- Windy ☐

WHAT I LIKED MOST:

MY TRIP TO:

THE WEATHER WAS:

Sunny ☐

Cloudy ☐

Rainy ☐

Windy ☐

FROM ............-............-............ (DATE)

TO ............-............-............ (DATE)

I WENT WITH ....(PERSONS)

WHAT I LIKED MOST:

MY TRIP TO:

THE WEATHER WAS:

- Sunny ☐
- Cloudy ☐
- Rainy ☐
- Windy ☐

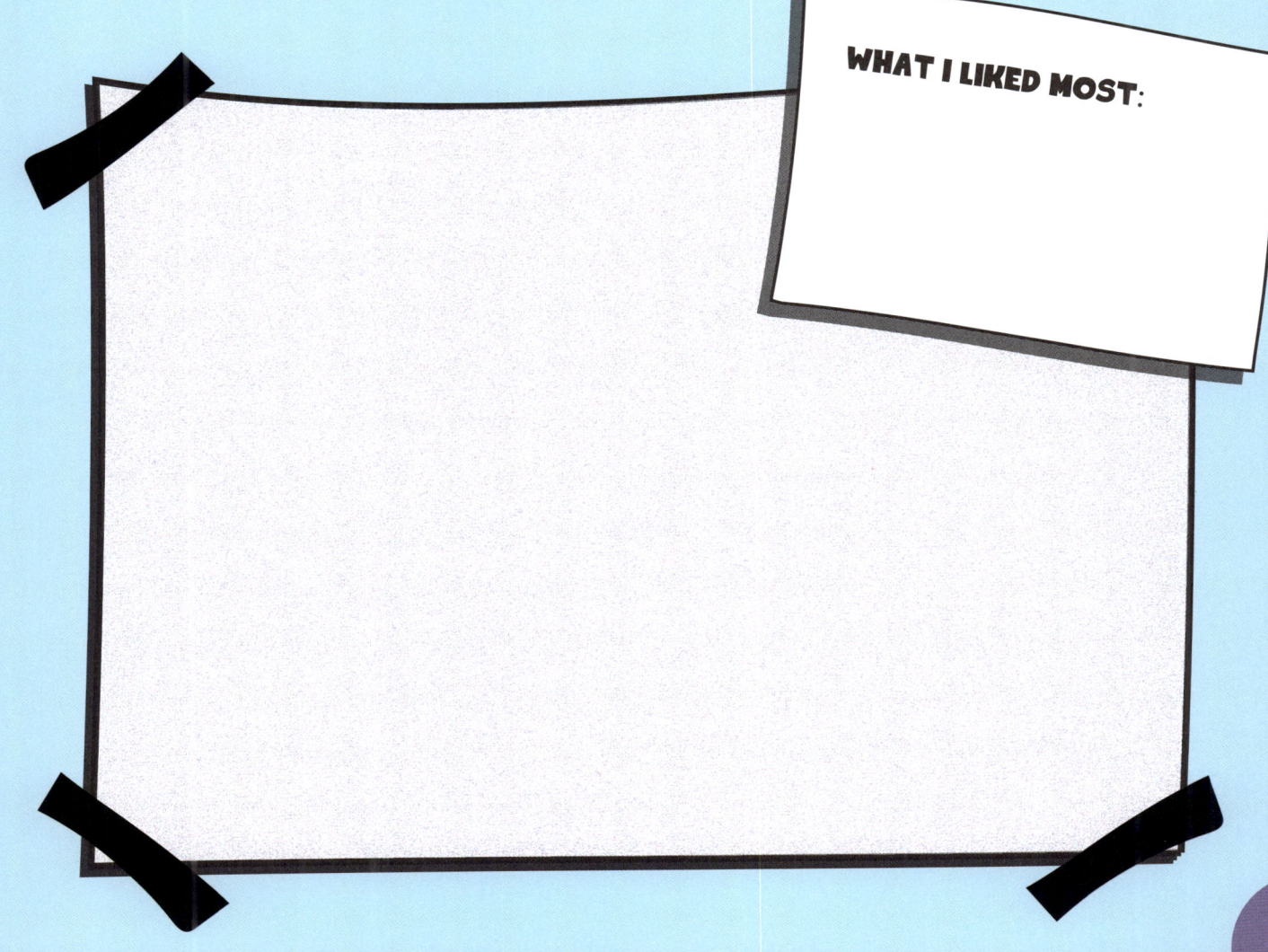

FROM ................-................-.................... (DATE)

TO ................-................-.................... (DATE)

I WENT WITH ....(PERSONS)

WHAT I LIKED MOST:

MY TRIP TO:

THE WEATHER WAS:

Sunny ☐
Cloudy ☐
Rainy ☐
Windy ☐

FROM ................-................-.................... (DATE)

TO ................-................-.................... (DATE)

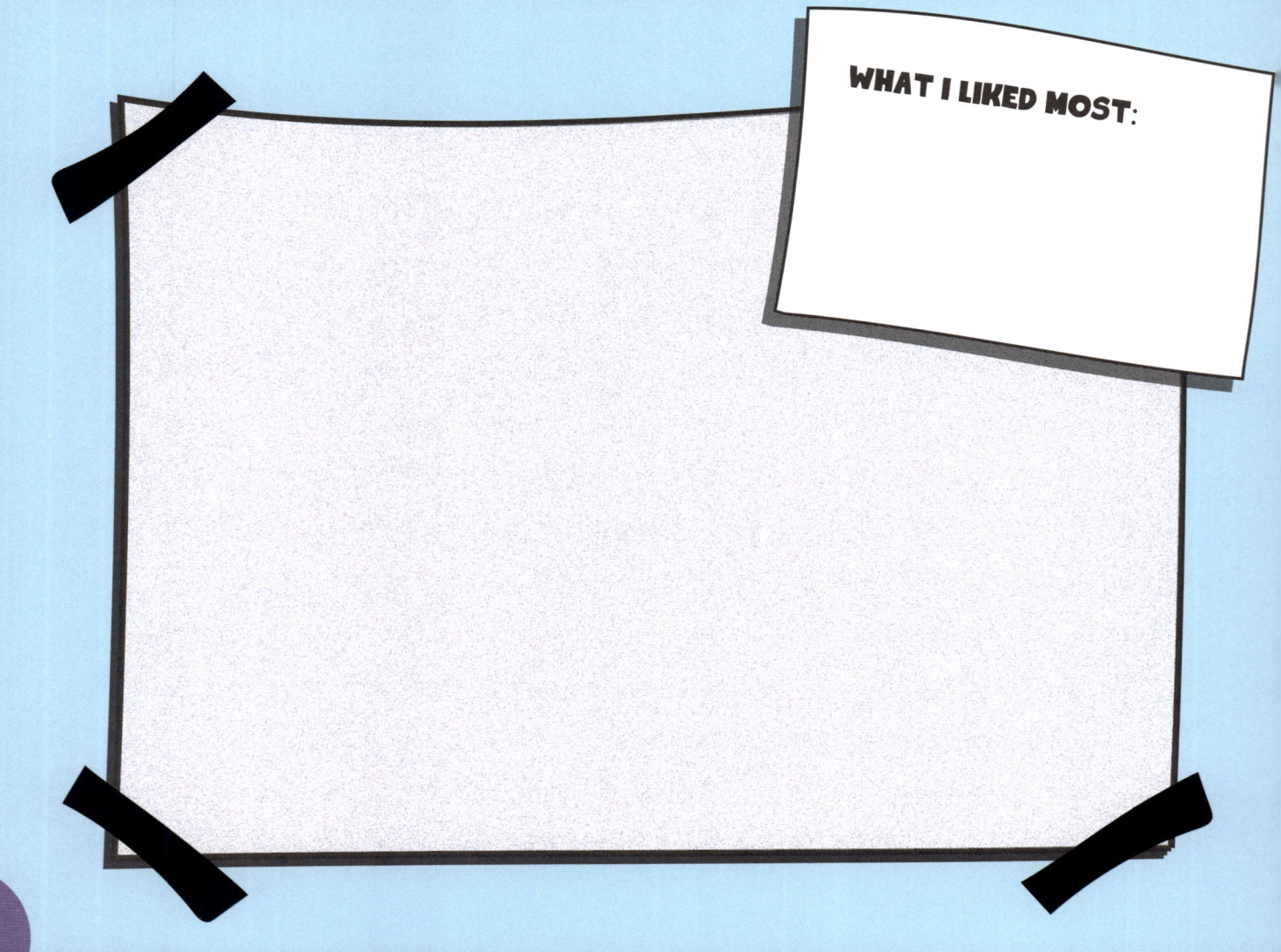

I WENT WITH ....(PERSONS)

WHAT I LIKED MOST:

MY TRIP TO:

FROM ................-................-................ (DATE)

TO ................-................-................ (DATE)

I WENT WITH ....(PERSONS)

THE WEATHER WAS:

Sunny ☐

Cloudy ☐

Rainy ☐

Windy ☐

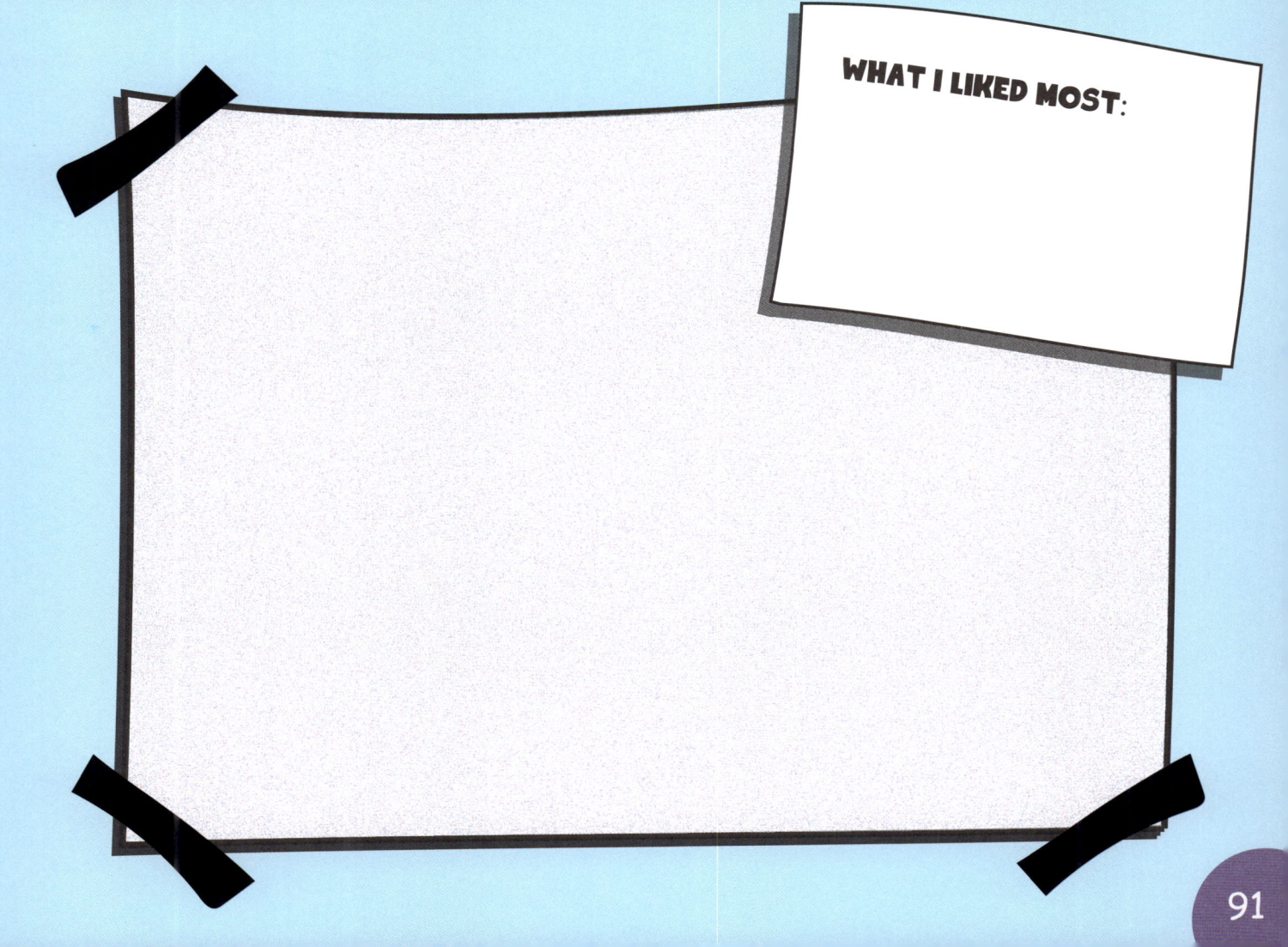

WHAT I LIKED MOST:

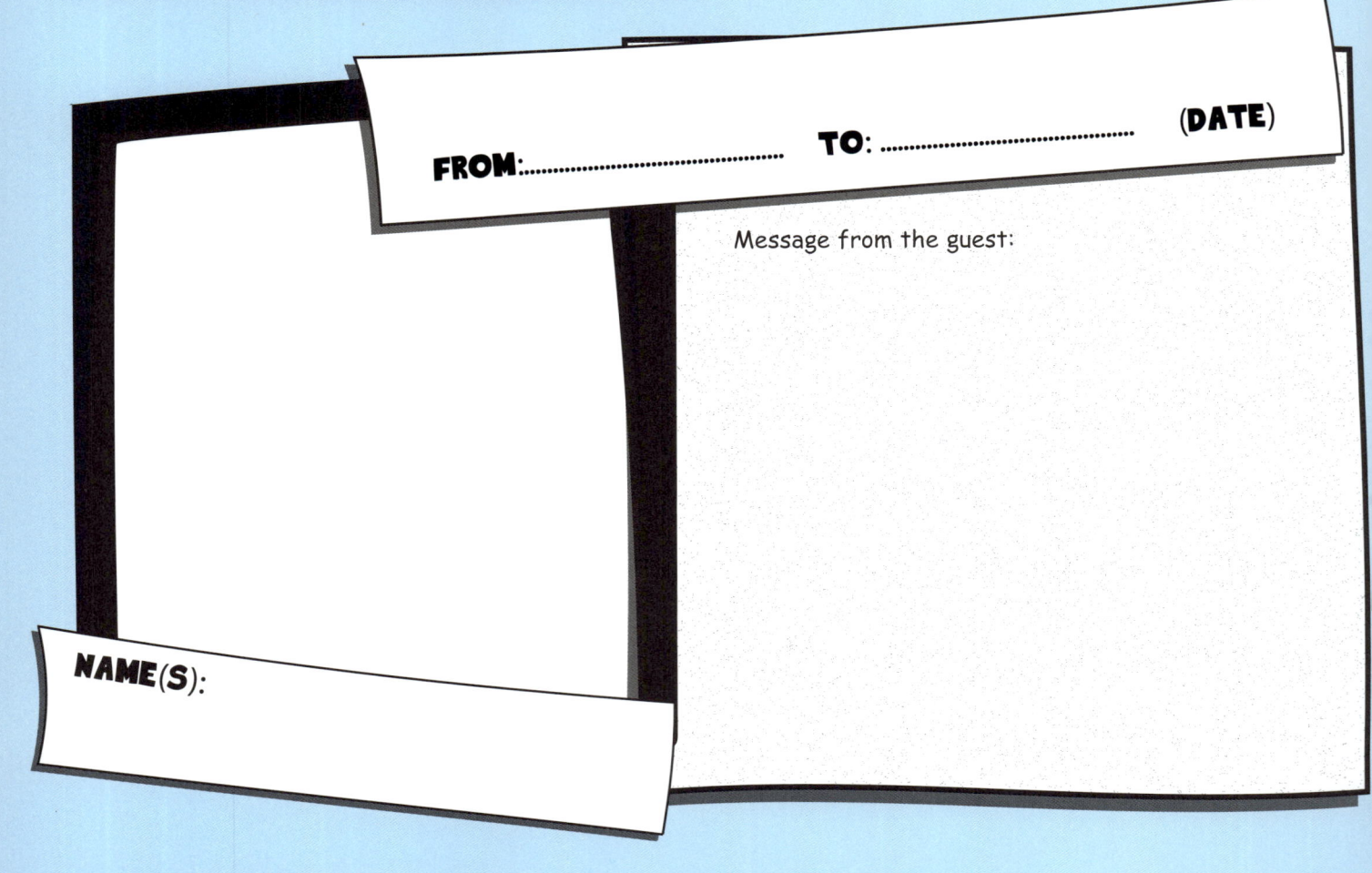

MY GUESTBOOK

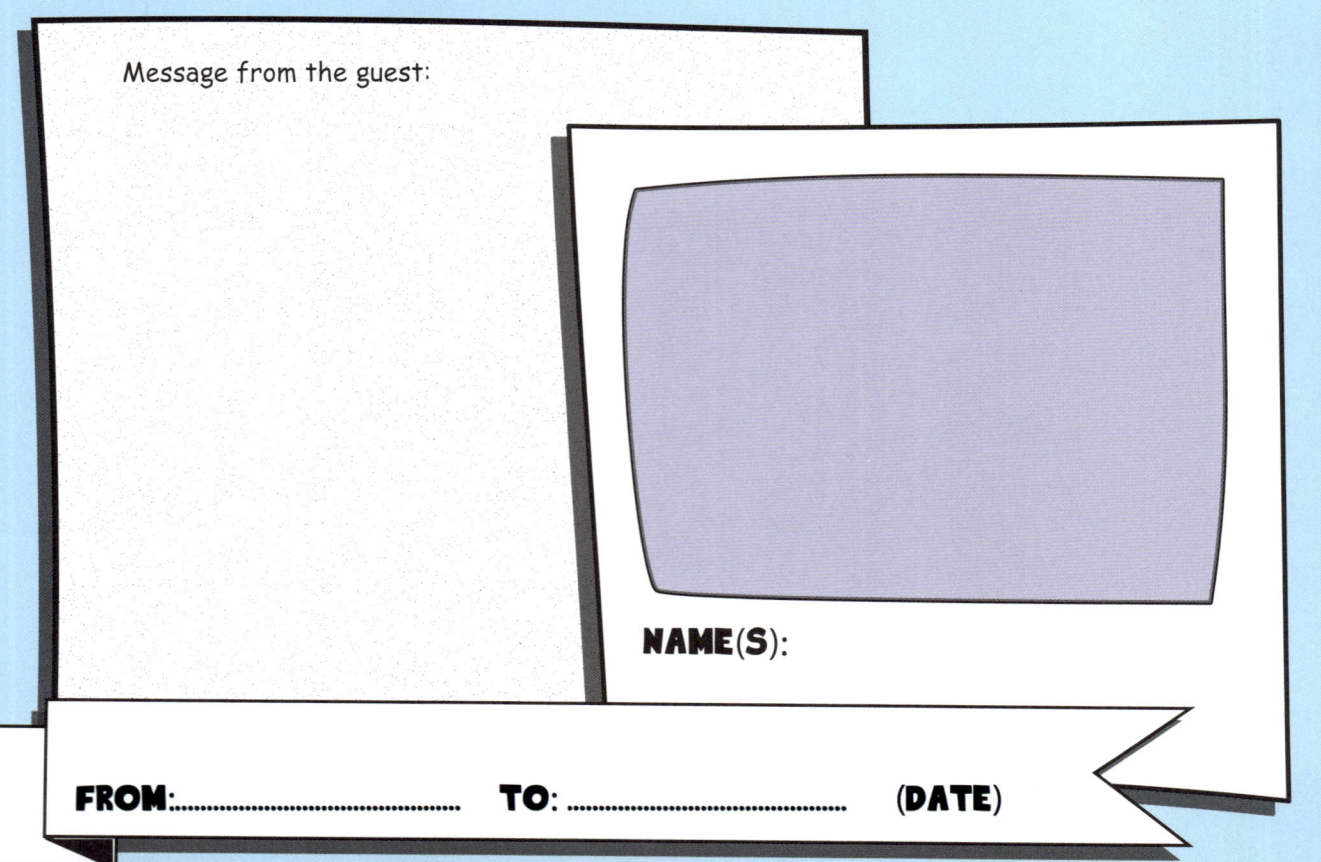

FROM:............................... TO: .... (DATE)

Message from the guest:

NAME(S):

Message from the guest:

NAME(S):

FROM:............................... TO: .... (DATE)

FROM:................................. TO: .... (DATE)

Message from the guest:

NAME(S):

FROM:................................. TO: .... (DATE)

Message from the guest:

NAME(S):

MY GUESTBOOK

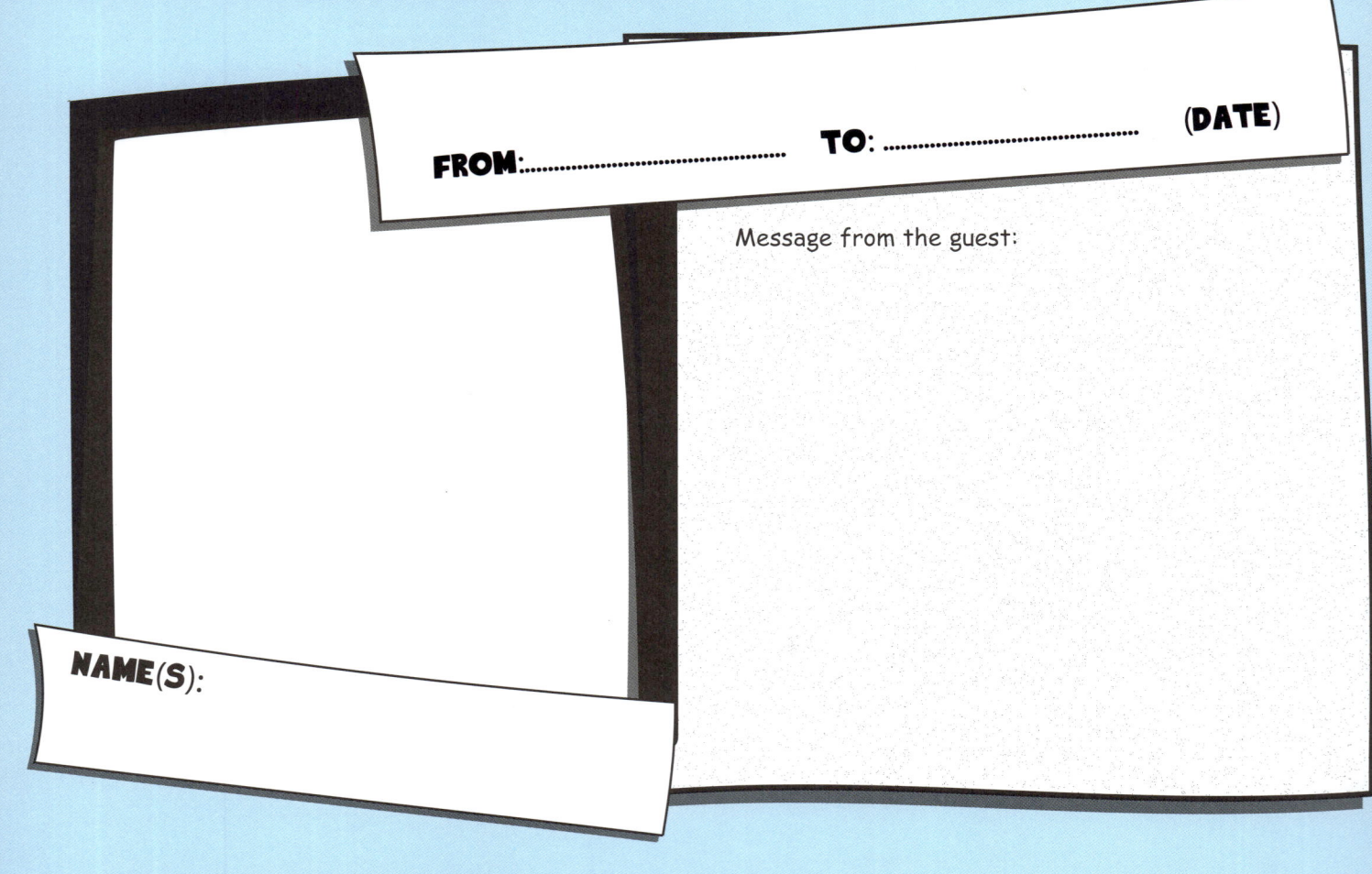

FROM:............................... TO: .... (DATE)

Message from the guest:

NAME(S):

Message from the guest:

NAME(S):

FROM:............................... TO: .... (DATE)

FROM:................................ TO: .... (DATE)

Message from the guest:

NAME(S):

FROM:................................ TO: .... (DATE)

Message from the guest:

NAME(S):

MY THOUGHTS

You can use these pages for your thoughts, memories, and stories.

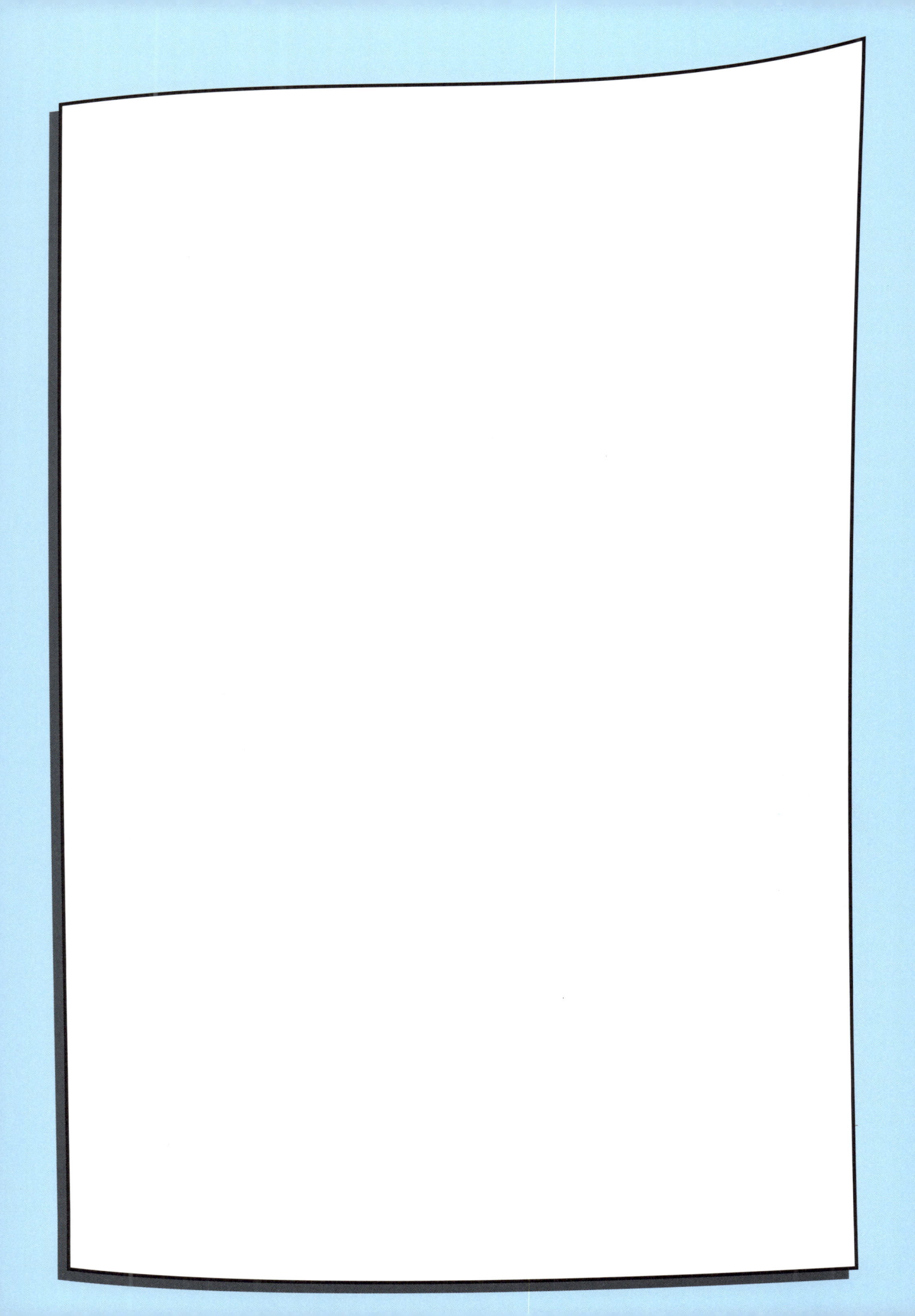

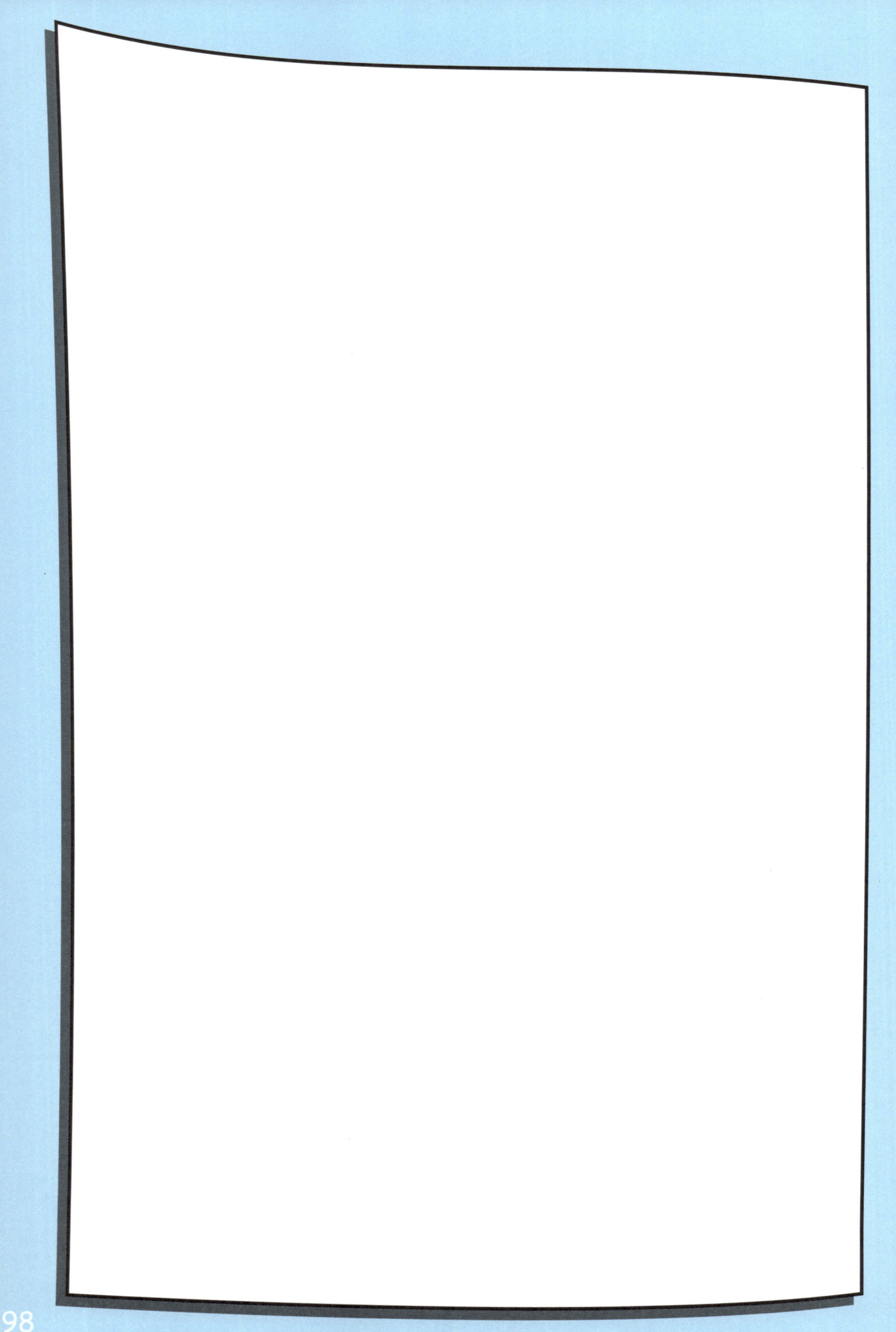

OUR EXPERTS

We would like to thank our dear friends, family, coaches, psychologists, parents, teachers, and children who helped us create this workbook. Thanks to your expertise, time, reviews, feedback, and enormous effort this book is a true guide for every child who has a Big Move.

A special big thanks to Manon de Bont, Julie de Widt, Carolien Batenburg-Soons, Carolien De Rooij-Sins, Mechteld Huijsmans, Marie Christofferson, Jenny Oxbrow, Jitske de Haan, Mr. Ron, Ralph & Mary Minor, Tony Easterlin, and Floor van Loon.

★ ★ ★

Let's highlight our experts because the book wouldn't be as valuable without their input and expertise:

Henrieke Timmer – Mindfulness coach for kids at Kidsfocusnow, mom of two kids, lived in The Hague & Redmond.

Emily Rogers – Coach at Expat Parenting Abroad, specialized in helping expat families, mom of two kids, lived in New Delhi, Chong Ching, Taipei & Auckland.

Silvia van Dooren - Teacher Dutch elementary school Seattle, with a MA in Developmental and Educational Psychology, mom of two kids, lived in Rotterdam, Vancouver & Redmond.

Emma Unsworth - Teacher Taipei European School, mom of two kids, lived in Stratford Upon Avon & Taipei.

Judith Soons - Certified NOBCO Coach specialized in stress managment and high sensitivity, lived in Heerlen, Rotterdam & Eindhoven.

Claudia Degen - Headmaster & Teacher Dutch elementary school in Taipei and Beijing, Happiness Life Coach, lived in Arnhem, Beijing & Taipei.

★ ★ ★

And a huge thanks to **all the little movers**. Thank you so much for your expert judgement!

KAAT NORA EMMA KEES FELINE THOAS
JULOTTE ESPEN MAUD TIES HANNA

KEEP TRACK

LOOK WHAT I DID!

After completing a page, mark the box with a sticker or a pencil.

6	7	8	9	10	11	16	17	18
19	20	21	22	23	27	28	29	30
31	32	33	34	35	40	41	42	43
44	45	46	47	48	49	50	51	52
53	54	55	56	57	62	63	64	65
66	67	68	69	70	71	76	77	78
79	80	81	86	87	88	89	90	91
92	93	94	95	WELL DONE!!				